I AM EVERY WOMAN

GOD'S LEADING LADIES
EMPOWERMENT MANUAL

DR. PAULINE KEY

Unless otherwise indicated all scriptural quotations are taken from the King James Version of the Bible.

I AM EVERY WOMAN:
GOD'S LEADING LADIES EMPOWERMENT MANUAL
COPYRIGHT © 2010
DR. PAULINE KEY

Printed in the United States of America

Library of Congress Catalog – in Publication Data

ISBN 978-0692454725

Published by:
Jabez Books Writers' Agency
(A Division of Clark's Consultant Group)
www.clarksconsultantgroup.com

I AM EVERY WOMAN:
GOD'S LEADING LADIES
EMPOWERMENT MANUAL

Psalms 144:12 ...that our daughters may be as corner stones, polished after the similitude of a palace.

The objectives of this workshop:

1. To equip women to walk in a manner worthy of the calling and to grow in the disciplines essential to triumph in spirit- filled living

2. To provide avenues for women to use their gifts to help fulfill the vision of her church home, and help to restore our homes, children, communities, nation and the world

3. To promote true sisterhood in the Body of Christ and bring healing, deliverance, purpose, and restoration to all women, enabling them with the necessary tools for effective women's ministry

This book originated from a workshop designed to teach and cultivate women's development in church ministry. It has significant topics that are essential in helping emerging churches with beginning women's and missions programs.

ABOUT the FACILITATOR --- Pauline Key, D.D.

As a minister of the Gospel for more than 18 years, Dr. Key's life mission is to advance the Kingdom of God through preaching/teaching the unadulterated Word of God; singing songs of His power to heal and deliver; and establishing works by co-laboring with the five-fold ministry gifts. Committed to serving God's people, this servant-disciple has a plethora of accomplishments on the spiritual battlefield:

*Christian Educator & Minister--Past instructor for the Potter's Institute Bible College, T. D. Jakes, Dallas, Texas; founder of Covenant Daughters Outreach Ministries serving the Dallas-Ft. Worth and Austin, Texas, and Detroit, Michigan areas. As a Youth Pastor established and coordinated a Youth Ministry for six years at Christ Abundant Life Ministries. Founded Seeds of Strength Youth Outreach Ministries; Worked with Pastor Bruce Burklow and Deon Sanders in establishing Youth Ministries; Founder and CEO of Kingdom Legacy Ministries and Served as a Crusade Event Coordinator and Life Coach for Ambassadors for Christ Ministries, a transitional ministry for men from all walks of life; Served with Bishop Eddie Long in rebuilding inner city communities. Served with SCLC "Justice For Girls" directed by Cathelean Steele.

*Business Woman and Entrepreneur—as an astute business woman and entrepreneur, founded Kingdom Awards -- Kingdom Awards acknowledges the accomplishments of men and women who have significantly contributed to enhancing the quality of life for others and has dedicated their lives to advancing the kingdom of God and impacting lives with the gospel message of Jesus Christ.

She is also the Founder of Esther's School of Beauty—a mentorship program for girls ages 10-17. Dr. Key has experience as account coordinator/trainer/business manager for some of the leading cosmetic lines in the industry. She is skilled as a licensed-certified cosmetologist, a Success Image Consultant and professional Celebrity Make-up Artist. She is co-author and developer of Business Development Initiative, Inc. an Entrepreneurship School for youth to acquire business and leadership skills inaccessible to them in the traditional school setting. She served as Executive Director of Georgia Minority Business Awards and the prestigious Gospel Choice Awards.

*Christian Television Hostess and Songstress -- Currently she is seen on TBN (Trinity Broadcasting Network) "Joy In Our Town" and WATC TV57 in Metro Atlanta with over 46 million viewers world-wide; has also appeared on numerous other television and radio shows. Her gift of singing catapulted her as a national and international recording artist, and named Best New Artist by the 2006 Gospel Choice Awards; Best Female Singer 2012 Gospel Choice Awards; appeared on nationwide television to sing for President Bill Clinton's 50th Birthday Celebration. She also performed for the MLK Memorial and the 50th Anniversary March on Washington Legacy Gala.

*Previous Publication—Author of Carriers of Vision: Redefining Womanhood (2001) Pray, Prey, Pray (2014) I Am Every Woman (2014)

*Other—on a personal note Dr. Key is the mother of three beautiful children. She attended University of Louisiana. She earned the Doctor of Divinity degree from Tabernacle Bible College in Miami, Florida in 2004.

I AM EVERY WOMAN

God's Leading Ladies Women Empowerment Manual

TABLE OF CONTENTS

Chapter One

The Church: God's Vision

I believe with all my heart that there is something in the heart and mind of God that he desires to reveal to those who are faithful in this time.

According to 1Samuel 2:35, he confirms it by saying, "Then I will raise up for myself a faithful priest who shall do according to what is in My Heart and in My Mind. I will build him a sure house and he shall walk before My anointed forever".

In these last days, God desires to prepare for himself a church whose garment is without spot or wrinkle, a chaste virgin, and a glorious church: One that would reveal His redemptive plan for mankind and convey the authenticity and the trustworthiness of the true gospel message to a world that is lost; and in search of the true and living God. In fulfilling His plan, God is looking to and fro to find someone to show Himself mighty through, priests (men and women) who will do what is in His heart to do.

I believe that women of God have an intricate part to play in fulfilling the plan of God. Now is the time, if any, that women must position themselves in Christ, meaning to take their place of influence in the body of Christ.

This manual will reveal where your true power and authority lie and empower you to release your authority in every role you play in life as women of God- mothers, sisters, wives, and business women. You will be strengthened with might by the power of the Holy Spirit to walk out your divine destiny as women with assurance and confidence. The Holy Spirit will unveil truths that will cause you to be effective messengers of the gospel to a lost world.

FAITHFULNESS

The faithfulness of God and His Word are a constant theme in the Bible. It is particularly prominent in Ps 89 and 119. God is "the faithful God who keeps covenant" (Deut 7:9) and chooses Israel (Isa 49:7); great is His faithfulness (Lam 3:23). These include dependability, loyalty, and stability particularly as it describes God in His relationship to human believers.

It is not surprising that this aspect of God's nature also belongs to the Messiah, who would be clothed with faithfulness (Isa 11:5) and who is described as the Faithful one (Rev 19:11), the "faithful witness"

(Rev 1:5; 3:14), and the "faithful High Priest" (Heb 2:17; 3:2).

God's faithfulness is the source of the Christian's deliverance from temptation (1 Cor. 10:13); assurance of salvation (Heb 10:23); and forgiveness of sins (1 John 1:9). He is faithful to His children because He is first of all faithful to Himself (2 Tim 2:13).

God's faithfulness should be so deeply reflected in the lives of His people (Gal 5:22) that they can be called simply "the faithful" (Ps 31:23). The Bible speaks of the faithfulness of Abraham (Neh. 9:8), Moses (Heb 3:5), and Paul (1 Cor. 7:25).

Faithfulness to one's fellowman is seen especially in relation to fulfilling an office. A steward must be found faithful (1 Cor. 4:2), just as Daniel and other persons in the Bible exercised their faithfulness toward God (Dan 6:4; 2 Tim 2:2). Today, faithfulness is also expected in Christian believers.

God always set aside a people for Himself
The Levites, God's chosen tribe were set apart for the service of God.

Num 3:11-13, And the Lord said to Moses, 12 "Look, I have chosen the Levites from among the Israelites to serve as substitutes for all the firstborn sons of the people of Israel. The Levites belong to me, 13 for all the firstborn males are mine. On the day I struck down all the firstborn sons of the Egyptians, I set apart for myself all the firstborn in Israel, both of people and of animals. They are mine; I am the Lord." NLT

LEVITES - Descendants of Levi: who served as assistants to the PRIESTS in the worship system of the nation of Israel. As a Levite, AARON and his sons and their descendants were charged with the responsibility of the priesthood offering, burnt offerings, and leading the people in worship and confession. All the other Levites who were not descended directly from Aaron were to serve as priestly assistants, taking care of the tabernacle and the Temple and performing other menial duties (Num 8:6).

The choice of the Levites as a people who would perform special service for God goes back to the days of the Exodus when the children of Israel were camped at Mount Sinai. The people grew restless while they waited for Moses to return from talking with the Lord on the mountain. Breaking their covenant with God, they made a golden calf and began to worship it.

 The Levites were no less guilty than the other tribes. But when Moses returned and called for those on the Lord's side to come forward, the descendants of Levi were the only ones who voluntarily rallied to his side, showing zeal for God's honor (Ex 32:26-28).

Even before this event, Aaron and his sons had been set apart for the priesthood. But many helpers were needed to attend to the needs of the tabernacle, which was built later at God's command in the Wilderness of Sinai. The Levites were chosen for this honor.

The designation of a tribe for special service to God grew out of an unusual concept of the Hebrew people known as the first fruits.

According to this principle, the first part of a crop to be harvested was dedicated to God. This principle even extended to the first children to be born in a family. Just before the Exodus from Egypt, when God sent the death angel to kill the firstborn of every Egyptian family, He instructed the Israelites to put blood on their doorposts, that their firstborn might be spared the same fate. Thus, the firstborn of every Israelite family became God's special property, dedicated to Him as a memorial. But because the Levites were the ones who voluntarily returned to their Lord after worshiping the golden image, they were chosen for service to the sanctuary, thus replacing the firstborn as God's representatives of the holiness of His people (Num 3:12-13,41).

Young Levites began as assistants to the priests and chief Levites, then progressed through the higher duties and offices such as doorkeeper, member of the Temple orchestra, or administrator.

In the days before the Temple was built and the people worshipped in the tabernacle, the Levites always transported the tabernacle and its furniture when the camp was moved. Then they erected and cared for the tent in its new location. They guarded it, cleaned it, and cleaned the furniture (Num 1:50-53; 3:6-9; 4:1-33).

Since the Levites served under the priests, they were forbidden to touch any sacred furniture or the altar until it had been covered by the priests (Num 4:15). Temple slaves often assisted the Levites in the heavier, more menial duties such as cutting wood and carrying water (Josh 9:21; Ezra 8:20).

The Levites also prepared the SHOWBREAD and did whatever baking was needed in connection with the sacrifices. They helped the priests slaughter and skin the animals for sacrifices, examined the lepers according to the Law, and led music during worship. Retiring from active service at age 50, the Levites were free to remain in the Temple as overseers or to give assistance to their young successors (Num 8:25-26).

Unlike the other tribes of Israel, the Levites received no territorial inheritance in the promised land of Canaan. Their portion was to be God Himself (Num 18:20), who commanded that 48 cities be set apart for them, along with enough pasture for their cattle (Num 35:1-8). They were to receive the tithes due God from the fruits of the fields, the flocks and herds, the fruits of the firstborn, and certain portions of the people's sacrificial offerings (Num 18:24). Of these tithes, the Levites had to turn over a tithe (a tenth part) to the priests (Num 18:26).

The Levites were not required to devote all their time to the sanctuary. During most of the year, they lived in their own cities. Then at fixed periods they came to the tabernacle to take their turn at work. For example, during David's reign, the Levites were divided into four classes: (1) assistants to priests in the work of the sanctuary, (2) judges and scribes, (3) gatekeepers, and (4) musicians. Each of these classes, with the possible exception of the second, was subdivided into 24 courses or families who served in rotation (1 Chron. 24-25; Ezra 6:18).

During the long period of Old Testament history, the Levites waxed hot and cold in their devotion to God, just like the rest of the nation of Israel. During the period of the judges, for example, a Levite agreed to hire his services to a man who was known as a worshiper of false gods (Judg. 17:8-13). By New Testament times, both Levites and priests presided over a form of worship that had lost its warmth and human concern (John 1:19)

In His parable of the Good Samaritan; Jesus insisted that true worship consisted of doing good to others. This is demonstrated by the lowly Samaritan traveler, who stopped to help a wounded man. What a contrast his compassion is to the hands-off approach of a priest and a Levite, both of whom "passed by on the other side" (Luke 10:31-3).

The Levites demonstrated the example of servant hood, a necessary quality in the church.

SERVANTHOOD is the act of one that honors others through giving, respect; *especially*: one that performs duties about the person or home of a master or personal employer. Faithfully submitting to the Word of God through obedience and worship of Him; helping and encouraging others to know Him through one's words and deeds.

Things to Ponder

1.   What thoughts and images come to mind when you think of the word servant? Are these mostly negative, mostly positive, or a good mixture of both?

2.   Decide together what you believe is the best definition for the word servant.

3.   Discuss how the following verses relate to servant hood. Look in a fresh way at each passage, searching especially for (a) God's commands and standards to keep, (b) someone's example to learn from, (c) a promise from God to believe, (d) a warning to heed, or (e) a challenge to face.

·   Matt 20:28
·   Luke 10:25-37
·   John 13:1-17; 15:15
·   Rom 15:8
·   Eph 6:5-8
·   Phil 2:5-8

4.   What vital, fundamental principles can you see in these passages (principles which are consistent with other Scriptures you know)?

5.   In conclusion, answer these questions, especially in light of what you've observed in the passages above: (a) what does God want me to understand most about Himself? (b) What does God want me to understand most about others? (c) What does God want me to understand most about myself? And in light of all this, what would He have me do?

Chapter Two

The Purpose of the Church

I. Definition of the Church

A local assembly of believers as well as the redeemed of all the ages who follow Jesus Christ as Savior and Lord. The Kingdom of God is established on earth through the church.

In the four gospels of the New Testament, the term church is found only in Matt 16:18 and 18:17. This scarcity of usage in those books that report on the life and ministry of Jesus is perhaps best explained by the fact that the church as the body of Christ did not begin until the day of PENTECOST after the ASCENSION of Jesus (Acts 1:1-4).

The day of Pentecost is the birthday of the Christian church. Prior to Pentecost, the people had been individual followers of Jesus. Animated by his spirit on the evening of Pentecost, the church was born with 3140 consisting of Apostles, previous disciples, and converts.

The church began on the day of Pentecost may be demonstrated in various ways: (1) Christ Himself declared the church to be yet future; (2) it was founded upon the death, resurrection, and ascension of Christ, and such an accomplished fact was not possible until Pentecost (Gal 3:23-25); (3) there could be no church until it was fully purchased with Christ's blood (Eph 1:20).

The Greek word for church is ekklesia. It originally meant an assembly called out by the magistrate, or by legitimate authority. It was in this last sense that the word was adapted and applied by the writers of the New Testament to the Christian congregation.

This word is used 115 times in the New Testament, mostly in the Book of Acts and the writings of the apostle Paul and the general epistles. **At least 92 times this word refers to a local congregation**. The other references are to the church general or all believers everywhere for all ages.

In the one Gospel of St. Matthew the church is spoken of no less than thirty-six times as "the kingdom." It is Christ's household, Matt 10:25; the salt and light of the world, Matt 5:13, 15; Christ's flock, Matt 26:31; John 10:15. Its members are the branches growing on Christ the Vine, John 15; But the general description of it, not metaphorical but direct, is that it is a kingdom, Matt 16:19.

When the church general is implied, church refers to all who follow Christ, without respect to locality or time. The most general reference to the church occurs in Eph 1:22; 3:10-21; 5:23-32. Since the church general refers to all believers of all ages, it will not be complete until after the judgment; and the assembly of all the redeemed in one place will become a reality only after the return of Christ (Heb 12:23; Rev 21:1-22:21).

Because the church general will not become a tangible reality until after Christ's return, the greatest emphasis in the New Testament is placed upon the idea of the local church. The local church is the visible operation of the church general in a given time and place.

The Great Commission Speaking to His followers after His resurrection, Jesus commissioned the church to make disciples and teach them what He had taught (Matt 28:16). The entire Book of Acts is the story of the early church's struggle to be loyal to this commission. As one reads this book, he is impressed by the reality that Christ, through the presence of the Holy Spirit, continues to direct His church as it carries out its commission.

Activities The early church met in the Temple and Jewish synagogues, as well as private homes of believers (Acts 5:42). Later, in recognition of Christ's resurrection on the first day of the week, Sunday became the principal time for public worship (1 Cor. 16:2). At these public worship services, missionary teachings and outreach in the name of Christ were offered to all within reach.

In the worship services of early Christians, prayer was offered, not only on the Lord's Day, but on special occasions as well (Acts 12:5), and Scripture was read (James 1:22; 1 Thess. 5:27). The breaking of bread and the sharing of the cup on the Lord's Day were observed as a continuing proclamation of Jesus' death, an anticipation of His return, and a participation in His "body and blood" (1 Cor. 11:20-29). Offerings for the needy were also received (1 Cor. 16:2).

Organization At first, church organization was flexible to meet changing needs. As the church became more established, however, church officers came into existence. These included the APOSTLES; PROPHETS; EVANGELISTS; ELDERS; BISHOPS; MINISTERS or teachers, DEACONS; and DEACONESSES.

Although church organization varies from denomination to denomination today, the pattern and purpose of the New Testament remains a model for churches as they pursue their mission in the world.

III. The Origin of the Church

In Acts 2:41, indirectly exhibited are the essential conditions of church communion. (Fellowship)
1) Baptism, implying on the part of the recipient repentance and faith
2) Apostolic Doctrine
3) Fellowship with the Apostles
4) The Lord's Supper
5) Public Worship. The real Church consists of all who belong to the Lord Jesus Christ as his disciples, and are one in love, character, hope, in Christ as the head of all; though as the body of Christ it consists of many parts.

The whole body of professing Christians throughout the world (1 Cor 15:9; Gal 1:13; Matt 16:18) are the church of Christ.

The church visible "consists of all those throughout the world that profess the true religion, together with their children." It is called "visible" because its members are known and its assemblies are public. Here there is a mixture of "wheat and chaff", of saints and sinners. "God has commanded his people to organize themselves into distinct visible ecclesiastical communities, with constitutions, laws, and officers, badges, ordinances, and discipline, for the great purpose of giving visibility to his kingdom, of making known the gospel of that kingdom, and of gathering in all its elect subjects. Each one of these distinct organized communities which is faithful to the great King is an integral part of the visible church, and all together constitutes the catholic or universal visible church. A credible profession of the true religion constitutes a person a member of this church. This is "the kingdom of heaven"' whose character and progress are set forth in the parables recorded in Matt 13.

The church invisible "consists of the whole number of the elect that have been, are, or shall be gathered into one under Christ, the head thereof." This is a pure society, the church in which Christ dwells. It is the body of Christ. It is called "invisible" because the greater part of those who constitute it are already in heaven or are yet unborn, and also its members still on earth cannot certainly be distinguished. The qualifications of membership in it are internal and are hidden. It is unseen except by Him who 'searches the heart'. "The Lord knoweth them that are his." (2 Tim 2:19).

The church, to which the attributes, prerogatives, and promises pertaining to Christ's kingdom belong, is a spiritual body consisting of all true believers... the church invisible.

(1.) **Unity**. God has only one church on earth. We sometimes speak of the Old Testament Church and of the New Testament church, but they are one and the same. The Old Testament church was not to be changed but enlarged (Isa 49:13-23; 60:1-14). When the Jews are at length restored, they will not enter a new church, but will be grafted again into "their own olive tree" (Rom 11:18-24; comp. Eph 2:11-22). The apostles did not set up a new organization. Under their ministry disciples were "added" to the "church" already existing (Acts 2:47).

(2.) **Universality**. It is the "catholic" church; not confined to any particular country or outward organization, but comprehending all believers throughout the whole world.

(3.) **Perpetuity**. It will continue through all ages to the end of the world. It can never be destroyed.

IV. Church Government

Church government is the organization pattern by which a church governs itself. At first, church organization and government in the New Testament was flexible to meet changing needs. But as the church became better established, it gave attention to the right structures and procedures that would help it accomplish its mission. In the earliest days, the APOSTLES directed the work of the church. Then seven men were chosen to assist the needs (Acts 6). Later, PROPHETS, EVANGELISTS, ELDERS, BISHOPS, and DEACONS were chosen.

Chapter Three

THE ROLE OF WOMEN IN THE CHURCH

God's incredible creation called WOMAN

To understand the role of women in the church, it is important to consider God's design of women; How women were regarded in the early church: How women were used in God's plan and vision: and how women were inclusive in Christ's mission and ministry.

From the Book of Genesis we know that God created humankind, both "male and female" (Gen 1:27; 5:2). Both were created in God's image and both were given the responsibility of exercising authority over God's creation. The man, Adam, was created before the woman. Realizing Adam needed companionship and a helper, God caused put him into a deep sleep. From him he took a rib and created a woman, Eve, "a helper comparable to him" (Gen 2:18, 20). Man is incomplete without woman. Because she is called a "helper" does not imply that she is inferior to man. The same Hebrew word translated as helper is used of God in His relationship to Israel (Ps 33:20; 70:5).

The culture that developed around the Israelites in ancient times did not always have this perspective of woman. Certain Old Testament passages tend to reflect an attitude that woman was little more than a thing and that a woman should be subordinate to man. This tendency prevailed before the coming of Christ. One of the Jewish prayers dated from that era declared, "I thank Thee that I am not a woman."

How does one reconcile these two seemingly opposing views? In Galatians Paul was stating a general principle that men and women were equal, just as the slave is equal to his master in the sight of God. However, Paul did not require or teach that the slaveholder had to release his slaves. In the same manner, Paul requested the women to be submissive to their husbands-to preserve order within the church and to be a witness to outsiders.

The apostle Paul wrote, "There is neither Jew nor Greek, there is neither slave nor free, there is neither male nor female; for you are all one in Christ Jesus" (Gal 3:28). Within the writings of Paul, however, other statements restrict women from participating in church leadership as freely as men. Women were to keep silent in church; they were to be submissive to the male leaders (1 Cor. 14:34-35; 1 Tim 2:11-12).

Jesus lived and taught a better way-the way of love. He allowed women to accompany Him and His disciples on their journeys (Luke 8:1-3). He talked with the Samaritan woman at Jacob's Well and led her to a conversion experience (John 4). Jesus did not think it strange that Mary sat at His feet, assuming the role of a disciple. In fact, He suggested to Martha that she should do likewise (Luke 10:38-42). Although the Jews segregated the women in both Temple and synagogue, the early church did not separate the congregation by gender (Acts 12:1-17; 1 Cor. 11:2-16).

The word "woman," as used in Matt 15:28; John 2:4 and 20:13-15, implies tenderness and courtesy and not disrespect. Only where revelation is known has woman functioned in her due place of honor assigned to her.

Some of the finest leaders in Israel were women, in spite of the fact that the culture was male-dominated. Military victories were sometimes won because of the courage of one woman (Judg. 4-5; 9:54; Est. 4:16). God revealed His Word through PROPHETESSES (Judg. 4:4; Luke 2:36; Acts 21:9). God used Priscilla and her husband Aquila to explain "the way of God more accurately" to Apollos the preacher (Acts 18:26). The heroes of faith mentioned in Heb 11 include Sarah (v. 11), Moses' mother, Jochebed (v. 23), and Rahab the harlot (v. 31).

Several women are mentioned in Scripture as having been endowed with prophetic gifts Miriam (Ex 15:20), Deborah (Judg. 4:4, 5), Huldah (2 Kings 22:14), Noadiah (Neh. 6:14), Anna (Luke 2:36, 37), and the daughters of Philip the evangelist (Acts 21:8, 9). Women are forbidden to teach publicly (1 Cor. 14:34, 35; 1 Tim 2:11, 12). Among the Hebrews it devolved upon women to prepare the meals for the household (Gen 18:6; 2 Sam 13:8), to attend to the work of spinning (Ex 35:26; Prov. 31:19), and making clothes (1 Sam 2:19; Prov. 31:21), to bring water from the well (Gen 24:15; 1 Sam 9:11), and to care for the flocks (Gen 29:6; Ex 2:16).

An inescapably blessed fact fills the Scriptures: God has ordained that every believer realize the significance of their mission and ministry as His servants. Gender is no restriction intended to limit significance or breath of dimension in living for or serving Christ: "I will pour out my Spirit upon your sons and daughters......upon your menservants and your maidservants" (Acts 2:17, 18)

Women of the Bible
How they speak to us today

When we allow ourselves to be empowered by God's will, we are able to generate goodness and accomplish work we could never dream of doing on our own. Sometimes we are resistant; we don't respond to His presence nor to the rush of His word breathed into our spirit. But, God will fulfill his plan for us to achieve His purpose, whether or not we willingly cooperate with Him.

Biblical women speak to us today. Their lives tell us about what happens when are resistant to God's will and get locked into hardhearted stubbornness that robs us of our potential to generate goodness. These women acknowledged God as the Supreme Ruler of the universe. They made an impact that has lasted thousands of years.

Today as women of God we must carry the torch to our generation and generations to come. It is my strong belief that if we can grasp a hold of their perspectives, then we too can leave a legacy for thousands of years to come.

Jesus is the same today, yesterday and forevermore. The same power he granted to them, he will do the same for us. We must affirm "I am Every Woman" in our time. My prayer is that as you read about each woman you will glean from her life the wisdom, tenacity, intellect, and fear of God for your own lives. I pray you will be inspired to do more for your home, local church, community, and nation and throughout the world.

EVE
The First Woman: A Redemptive Instrument

[Eve] (Life-giving) - The first woman (Gen 3:20; 4:1), created from one of Adam's ribs to be "a helper comparable to him" (Gen 2:18-22).The name given by Adam to his wife (Gen 3:20; 4:1). The account of her creation is given in Gen 2:21, 22. By the Creator, by declaring that it was not good for man to be alone, and by creating for him a suitable companion, gave sanction to monogamy.

Helpmeet is a military term which means "weapon of mass destruction". "This companion was taken from his side to signify that she was to be dear unto him as his own flesh. She was not from his head, lest she should rule over him; nor from his feet, lest he should tyrannize over her; but from his side, to denote that species of equality which is to subsist in the marriage state." And again, "That wife that is of God's making by special grace, and of God's bringing by special providence, is likely to prove a helpmeet to her husband." Through the subtle temptation of the serpent she violated the commandment of God by taking of the forbidden fruit, which she gave also unto her husband (1 Tim 2:13-15; 2 Cor. 11:3).

Adam and Eve lived together in innocence and happiness, enjoying sexual union ("one flesh") without guilt and sin (Gen 2:25). However, the serpent tempted Eve to eat of the forbidden fruit (Gen 2:17).

Eve succumbed to the serpent's temptation and ate the forbidden fruit. Then, "she also gave to her husband with her, and he ate" (Gen 3:6). The result of this disobedience was the loss of innocence and the disturbing knowledge of sin and evil. "Then the eyes of both of them were opened, and they knew that they were naked; and they sewed fig leaves together and made themselves coverings" (Gen 3:7) to conceal their shame.

In falling to temptation (Gen 3:6), Eve knew sin and death (Gen 2:17). She and her descendants experienced the animosity between Satan and Christ-the "seed of the serpent" and "the seed of the woman" (Gen 3:15). Her pain in childbirth and Adam's authority over her were other results of her sin (Gen 3:16).

The apostle Paul referred to Eve twice. By saying "the serpent deceived Eve by his craftiness," Paul gave an example of how easily a person can be led into temptation and sin, with disastrous consequences (2 Cor. 11:3; 1 Tim 2:12-14).

It is a remarkable token of divine grace that God, in His mercy and in His giving of the first promise to become an instrument of Gods redemptive working. Eve's distinct place I the failure of the first couple becomes the soil in which god's mercy plants the first seed of promise. The message is obvious: God is able to make all grace abound toward any of us. However deep the failure, Eve testimony declares God's grace goes deeper yet.

ESTHER
Rising to meet your destiny

The Hebrew name for Esther, "Hadassah" means myrtle, referring to a beautiful evergreen shrub. {There was something else you said, I can't remember.}

Queen Esther, orphaned as a Jewish girl, and raised by her uncle Mordecai grew into a beautiful woman to become queen to King Xerxes. It was not revealed to the king that his queen was a Jew. Though her life embraced recognition, success, wealth, luxury—an environment many may covet—Esther was a woman of deep perspective and integrity. She understood the power of prayer and fasting; recognizing the reality of the spiritual realm and the Holy Spirit resources (4:16).

As the story goes, Haman a man of low morals and contempt had influence upon the king. Haman persuaded King Xerxes to sign an edict to destroy all the Jews in his extensive kingdom. Mordecai her unforgotten uncle sent a message to Esther urging her to tell the king she was Jewish and to speak up for all the Jews in the kingdom so her people would be spared. Esther must have been terrified, wondering what the king would do to her when he found out her heritage.

During this time no one was allowed to approach the king unless he or she was invited. If the king did not extend his gold scepter to someone who showed up at his throne room uninvited, that person would be put to death. Perceiving a challenge and understanding that her life and that of her people were in jeopardy, Esther dared to go to the king.

As she gathered courage to make this surprise visit; Esther sent a message to Mordecai; directing him to have all the Jews to pray and fast as she would do for three days. She told him, "then I will go to the king even though it is against the law. And if I perish, I perish." (4:16) she appeared before the king, appealed to him and the Jews were saved.

Esther inspires us to act boldly and speak bravely for what we know is right and just. God opens destiny to any person who will keep and honor His priorities.

DEBORAH
Wife, Prophetess, and Leader of the Israelites
(Judge 4:4, 5)

Deborah- *The Spirit-filled, Multitalented Woman, and Prophetess* Deborah literally means "Bee", reminding us of this woman's wisdom, how she liberally shared with her friends, and how her influence and authority were used by God to sting Israel's enemies.

As a wife, Deborah was not only a helpmeet to her husband, but also a helper to mankind. Remember, Help meet is derived from a military term which means "a weapon of mass destruction". She might be called the first woman military commander and first female Supreme Court Justice!

As a Songstress, Deborah wrote songs of victory while in battle and sang them (Chapter 5). She was blessed with creative talents and leadership abilities that distinguished her as a patriotic woman of God who was a judge and led Israel for forty years. The bible describes an incident that shows how wise Deborah was as she "held court...in the hill country of Ephraim. The Israelites came to Deborah for wise counsel and sound judgments.

As a *leader of the Israelites* when for twenty years, the Israelites had been cruelly oppressed by tyrant Jabin, king of Canaan (judges 4-5) whose army, commanded by the powerful Sisera, included" nine hundred iron chariots, and was considered the weapons of mass destruction of their day. Deborah wasn't afraid of that army and its chariots Deborah were brave. Her bravery came from what she knew: that God was with her and that he would guide her in using her brains and her resources to do His will.

She called in a man named Barak and relayed to him God's directions to lead ten thousand Israelites to battle against Sisera. Barak answered, "If you go with me, I will go; but if you don't go with me, I won't go". (Judges 4:8) with her assurance, She appointed him as her field commander and assigned him the task of recruiting an army to defeat Sisera. Deborah also had the help of another brave woman, Jael, as she did so. Jael drove a tent peg through a villain's head to do what needed to be done (see Judges 4:17-22).

Deborah convinced her followers to extend themselves beyond their own vision. As an inspirational leader, Deborah provided a model of integrity and courage and sets a high standard of performance. She gave her followers autonomy and not only treats them as individuals, but encouraged individualism. There is no better way to develop leadership that to give an individual a job involving responsibility and let him work it out. Deborah did this with young Barak She was not afraid to set the example of courage and heroism by using herself as bait for the ambush.

The keys to Deborah's effectiveness were her spiritual commitment and walk with God. She demonstrated the possibilities for any woman today who will allow the spirit of God to fill and form her life, developing her full capacities to shape the world around her.

ABIGAIL
(1Samuel 25:23-24)

This Old Testament woman was married to Nabal, a wicked and foolish man... Abigail had the ability to defuse explosive situations. She could say a few words and ease the wrath of someone who was out for vengeance.

The Bible account is that prior to David becoming king; he and his men had associated with Nabal's shepherds by providing them protection and other services in return for food. Nabal hurled insults at David and slandered him. David became furious at the injustice. Abigail had nothing to do with Nabal's ridiculous and thoughtless actions; but upon hearing what had happened she knew David would be justified in killing her husband and destroying their entire household.

Risking her own life, she hurried to intercept David before he could carry out his revenge. 1Samuel 25: 23-24 records how she passionately took the blame for her foolish husband's actions.

When Abigail approached David, she quickly bowed down before David with her face to the ground. She fell at his feet and said: "My Lord, let the blame be on me alone. Please let your servant speak to you; hear what your servant has to say."

Abigail went on to praise David and remind him that he represented the Lord in the battles he fought and that someday when he was ruler over Israel he would regret the vengeful killing he was about to do.

Abigail's plea shows us that she was aware of something we would do well to heed today. She already knew what David's own son Solomon, who was yet unborn, would write many years later: "a gentle answer turns away wrath". (Proverbs 15:1)

This is one of several instances in scripture where strong and extremely capable women are used by God in crucial situations. Abigail certainly shows herself worthy to be a queen, with courage and grit, standing in stark contrast with Nabal "the fool".

.

QUEEN OF SHEBA
(1Kings 10:6-7)

Queen of Sheba longed *to seek out Wisdom*- having heard about a wise man called Solomon; his sayings and his wisdom, she desired to sit at his feet and learn from him. Hungry for the wisdom Solomon possessed, she traveled a long way to be mesmerized and overcome by what he taught her. Later Jesus would say,"she came from a far corner of the earth: (Matt 12:41)- To seek it out. She said to him, "it was a true report which I heard in my own land about your words and your wisdom". However, I did not believe the words until I came and saw with my own eyes; and indeed the half was not told. Your wisdom and prosperity exceed the fame of which I heard" (1Kings 10: 6-7). Later Jesus would say she came from a far corner of the earth (Matt 12:41) - to seek it out.

Queen of Sheba gave Solomon many, many gifts in gratitude for sharing his wisdom with her. We must believe that the queen took home the wisdom Solomon gave her and she used it to revolutionize her nation.

ANNA
Widow, Intercessor, and Prophetess
(Luke 2:36-38)

Anna = *a woman of insight*- Luke 2: 29-30, The name Anna means "Favor" or "Grace" and originates from the Hebrew Chanan, meaning "to bend or stoop in kindness" and "to find favor and show favor."

Anna the prophetess came from the tribe of Asher, the tribe that was to be blessed and that was to "dip his foot in oil" (Deut 33:24) – a sign of joy and happiness. But also, Asher's descendants were to have shoes of "iron and bronze", denoting strength (Deut33:25).

She found favor in God's eyes as he revealed the messiah, the Hope of Israel, to her aged eyes. Anna could see the Messiah in that sweet baby's face; and she told others what she had seen. Her prophetic anointing was untainted by the spirit of the age. Her historic prophecy regarding Jesus called attention of all present to the uniqueness of the child being brought into the temple for dedication (v22).

Her anointed ministry during later years of life holds forth a promise for older women. There is always ministry awaiting the sensitive, and obedient, who can influence and shape the rising generation. Anna, a widow, was an effective older woman.

Anna exemplified these qualities of anointing and steadfastness. After being married only seven years, her husband died, and this widow chose a life of fasting and prayer in the temple. She "did not depart from the temple, but served God", (Luke2:36, 37), clearly walking in moral purity and dedicated service.

MARY MAGDALENE
Freed to become fruitful
(Luke 8:2)

Mixed views characterize this woman from the town of Magdala. Some say she was a prostitute; she's been confused with the sinful woman forgiven by Jesus; and others believe she was the woman who broke the alabaster box of perfumed ointment. (Mark14:3-9)

Despite these varied depictions, scriptures reveal her love of the Lord was profound. Mary Magdalene first appears in the Gospels among a core group of women who assisted Jesus in His ministry. It is reported that she had been delivered from the bondage of seven demons. Because she had been freed from a terrible torment, she was diligent in her service to Christ, evidence of her gratitude.

She was present at his burial (Matt.27:55,56), and in the midst of those who came early Sunday (Easter) morning to complete the embalming of Jesus' body. (Mark 16:1) Upon hearing the angelic announcement of Jesus' resurrection (Mark 16:6) Mary Magdalene was the first person to talk to Him after He had arisen. (John 20:11-15)

It is foolish to conclude that her movement toward greeting Jesus with an embrace following the resurrection suggests anything other than pure joy at the discovery of Him being alive! Jesus' directive not to do so was not a signal she was unworthy in her approach. His words apparently indicated some yet uncompleted aspect of His post crucifixion mission.

Mary Magdalene was a thankful and steadfast disciple of Jesus. This can best be viewed as a case study of how no dimension of satanic bondage can prohibit an individual's being released to do fruitful service for Jesus Christ.

JOCHEBED, MIRIAM, PHARAOH'S DAUGHTER, SHIPHRAH, PUAH
Women of Valor

No wonder Moses was in God's plan to develop into a magnificent Man of God! His life was saved and molded by some extraordinarily wise, clever and courageous women: Jochebed his mother; Miriam his sister; Pharaoh's daughter who rescued him; and Shiphrah and Puah Hebrew midwives.

Pharaoh the leader of Egypt believed his enslaved Jews were becoming too populous and potentially more powerful. To alleviate what he perceived a threat to his kingdom, he planned to commit infanticide by instructing the midwives to kill all baby boys at birth. It is unsure whether they attended Jochebed when she gave birth; but we do know the midwives feared God and did not follow the orders of Pharaoh---they allowed the baby boys to live. (Exodus 1:17) When ole Pharaoh questioned why there were still so many little Hebrew boys cooing and gurgling in 'slave town'; they feigned innocence saying, "Hebrew women are not like Egyptian women, they are vigorous and give birth before the midwife arrives." (Exodus)

Although the midwives may not have delivered Moses, surely their actions may have inspired Jochebed to be ingenious and take steps to protect her baby son's life; hiding him for three months. No longer able to keep him hidden; she crafted a basket and placed him in it among some reeds along the bank of the River Nile. His sister Miriam was positioned at a distance to watch for what would happen to him. Pharaoh's daughter happened to go down to the Nile to bathe. Walking with her attendants along the riverbank; she saw the basket and sent her female slave to get it. Upon opening the basket, she saw the crying baby and felt sorry for him remarking, "This is one of the Hebrew babies." (Exodus 2:5, 6)

Then Miriam appeared and asked Pharaoh's daughter, "Shall I go and get one of the Hebrew women to nurse the baby for you?" "Yes, go." She answered. So the girl went and returned with her mother. Pharaoh's daughter said to Jochebed, "take this baby and nurse him for me and I will pay you." She took the baby and nursed him until he was older; then returned him to Pharaoh's daughter becoming her son. She named him Moses saying, "I drew him out of the water." (Exodus 2:7-10) Moses became a man living under the rule of the Egyptians.

All of these women were instrumental in God's design to bring up a leader for deliverance of His people.

ZIPPORAH
The feisty go getter
(Exodus 4:24-26)

This was a woman who loved her family and was especially close to her father, Jethro. A hard working woman she entered into an interracial marriage. As a black Ethiopian woman, she married a Hebrew man, Moses. She was determined to learn about his culture and understand his heart.

God directed Moses to return to Egypt. Reluctantly, he heeded God's instruction to go to free the Israelites taking Zipporah and their two sons with him.

Although Zipporah, was not a Jew, she understood the right of circumcision of boys which Moses had ignored. This displeased God and He was provoked to kill Moses. Then she took it upon herself to do what had to be done to save her husband from God's wrath. Zipporah took a sharp stone and cut off the foreskin of her son and cast it at Moses feet, and said, "Surely you are a husband of blood to me!" So He let him go. Then she said, "You are a husband of blood to me!"- Because of the circumcision .So (Exodus 4: 24-26)

Can you imagine how upset Zipporah was, having to do something so hurtful to her son... to save her husband? She did what had to be done. Moses may have been embarrassed because his wife did what he should have done. But embarrassment is better than death. We can learn from this strong-willed woman who crossed cultures and stood by her man, even when he couldn't stand up for his own beliefs.

LEAH AND RACHEL
(Gen 29:20-26)

The story of Leah and Rachel shows us how biblical women had survived broken hearts and what they had learned from their experiences. Some of the most notable stories of heartache occurred because of a woman's deepest unfulfilled longings.

Leah and Rachel longed to have what the other already possessed. Leah and Rachel were sisters married to the same man, their cousin Jacob, who actually wanted to marry Rachel. But the girl's father tricked Jacob into marrying Leah.

Jacob eventually married Rachel too and loved Rachael more than Leah. (v30) Rachel was unable to bare children early in the early part of her marriage but she bore two sons in later years and Leah bore many.

HANNAH
The Barren Woman

Hannah *was another barren woman who longed to be a mother*. Married to Elkanh, a man with two wives, though childless, she was his favorite. The other wife, Peninnah, was able to bare children. 1Samuel 1, describes an unhappy household and labels Peninnah as Hannah's rival; constantly provoking uppishly as she held it over her that *she* could bear children (v6)

Hannah, a faithful woman, was not annoyed by the pestering of her rival. Desiring to have a child, she turned to the Lord earnestly praying ," O Lord Almighty , if you will only look upon your servant's misery and remember me and not forget your servant but give her a son, then I will give him to the Lord for all the days of his life." Though mocked at times some considered her to be drunk as she prayed and worshipped the Lord; she conceived and a child was born unto her. She called him Samuel, because I asked him of the Lord.

We learn from Hannah to incorporate courage and faith into our lives so that it is a continual, empowering presence in our hearts. God enabled Hannah to conceive and give up the child who was most precious to her.

When we face seemingly impossible situations we believe without a doubt that our all-powerful God brings us through according to His will.

When illness steals our health or setbacks take our wealth or disability impedes our independence, we praise and cling to the God who is able to take us from barrenness to fruitfulness.

RAHAB
A Harlot Heroine
Joshua 2:1

It is clear how God viewed Rahab; we know He recognized her potential because of her faith. Through her- a heathen harlot- would form the lineage of the Messiah, God's own son (Matt 1:5)

It doesn't matter what is in your family line, God can use you.

BATHSHEBA
A King's Mistress
2 Samuel 11:2

We might be a little suspicious of Bathsheba's character in the beginning of this story, but the more we study her, the more we see her wisdom and her strong love for God.

Many scholars believe she was the mother of Lemuel, as well as Solomon. She is thought to be the original source of the inspiring description and instructional advice in Proverbs 31. If indeed, this was the case, we have to believe that she was passing on knowledge she learned the hard way through her own tragic experience. This woman knew a lot about life, marriage, and virtue. God responded to the adulterous relationship of David and Bathsheba with justice (the heartbreaking death of their child) but also with extravagant grace. He washed away their sin in a tidal wave of love and blessed them with more children, one of whom would carry on the lineage of the Messiah. Read Romans 5:20-21.

JEZEBEL
The Queen of Terror

Jezebel- *the queen of terror*- somehow this heathen nightmare of a woman became queen of Israel, where she wreaked terror and death on her people. The bible's commentary says "she committed many atrocious crimes to those who were faithful and obedient to God". Reading their story in the books of 1 and 2 Kings, we see the harmful characteristics of this evil woman; and we learn strong lessons from her wicked ways. She led her husband astray, converting him from his God-fearing faith to worship the heathen god, Baal. Oh sisters, be careful never to lead our love ones away from the almighty and all-powerful God! Make sure we steer completely clear of any remotely evil influences that our family members might see us reading, watching, listening or participating in acts that may cause them to mistakenly assume we endorse that kind of wicked behavior.

Further, ensure we don't fall for the enticement s of idols. While Baal may not be a common threat to today's believers, there are plenty idols of distraction- fame, money, possessions, status, relationships, or other nuisances that plants little seeds of discontent and discord which we may pass on- intentionally or unintentionally- to others.

Unlike Jezebel, Let us be a positive force in our husband's lives encouraging them to exude goodness and mercy toward all those around them. Avoid her evil ways, being especially careful not to take on a controlling spirit at home or wherever we go.

SARAH
Submission that Bears Fruit
Gen 16:1

Originally called, "Sarai", God changed Sarai's name to "Sarah "meaning Princess or Queen". This linked her in co-rulership with her husband Abraham (formerly Abram), the Father of many nations including her in His covenant promise (Genesis 17:15, 16).

Sarah was barren (16:1), a condition considered a curse in the ancient world. She is a positive lesson in faith that rises above personal limitations (Heb11:11) and in a submitted spirit that responds biblically to her husband, without becoming depersonalized (1Pet 3:5, 6).

Sarah is also an illustration of the dangers of taking God's promises into our own hands. Her suggestion that Abraham take her handmaid, Haggar, as wife, in view of Sarah's barrenness, resulted in the birth of Ishmael- a child who occasioned jealousy and dissension between the two women. This conflict became so strong that Abraham at the insistence of Sarah, sent Ishmael and Haggar away. With subsequent nations formed and the conflict of generations continues to this day.

RUTH
Tenacity that takes the Throne
Ruth 1:1-4:22

Ruth literally means "Friendship" or female friend. Nowhere else in the Bible do we find a lovelier picture of a true and loyal friend. Ruth's primary virtue is tenacity to purpose. She was a woman who was steadfast woman, constant in her commitment to her mother-in- law and tireless as she gleaned in the fields. The result of this constancy is her marriage to Boaz and the birth of Obed, who became the father of Jesse, whose son was David the King. Moreover, since Jesus was born of the seed of David, we see how Ruth, the alien Moabite, became part of the lineage of the Messiah.

HULDAH
2 Kings 22:3-20

The name "Huldah" is derived from the Hebrew root word "cheled", which means to glide swiftly. Perhaps Huldah's name reflects her quickness of mind and her ability to swiftly and rightly discern the things of God. In any case, this woman was used by God a fleeting moment in history to voice His judgment and His prophecy, and to spark one of the greatest national revivals in history. She is a case study of the character and the potential of a woman who today will receive the Holy Spirit's fullness and step through whatever open door God provides. It is worth observing how Hilkiah the high priest and Shaphan the scribe sought out Huldah for God's word of wisdom. Clearly, she gained the complete respect and confidence of these men, a lesson in the truth that spiritual influence flows from a spiritual life-style, not merely from the presence of spiritual gifts. Acts 2: 17, 18, promise that the church age allows for a proliferation of the Holy Spirit's anointing upon women. Let Huldah's example of respectful, trust-begetting, forthright living teach the grounds for wise and effective spiritual ministry.

REBEKAH
The blessings of an Unselfish Woman
Gen 24:15-67

Rebekah, the Syrian, was the granddaughter of Nahor, Abraham's brother. Rebekah's name refers to tying or binding up, implying that her beauty was so great, it could literally captivate or fascinate men. She is introduced as a diligently industrious and beautifully sensitive girl. Her willingness to serve Eleazar and her readiness to draw water for all of the thirsty camels dramatize this. A lesson in the way God provides surprising rewards for servant spirited souls is seen in what happened to Rebekah. Little did she know those camels were carrying untold gifts for her and her family. Her willing to wait for her family's blessing before accepting the invitation to leave for a marriage to Isaac, a wealthy prince of the ancient world, is a model for modern society. How many marriages today would be different 1) If the Holy Spirit were the guide, 2) if prayer and worship were the order of the day; and 3) If the couple were secure in the blessing of the family?

DAUGHTERS OF ZELOPHEHAD
A Godly Quest for Equal Rights
Numbers 27:1-11

Zelophehad, of the tribe of Manasseh, had five daughters and no sons. Their names were Mahlah, meaning "sickness or disease"; Noah, meaning "rest or comfort": Hoglah, meaning" partridge or boxer"; Milcah, meaning "queen or counsel"; and Tirzah, meaning "pleasantness". If we accept these women's names as pictures of their abilities, natures, or the adversities they overcame, we see all the qualities necessary for the tenacity, tact, courage, wisdom, and grace they needed to request and receive an inheritance for themselves.

Their presentation of their case to Moses and the leaders of Israel when the land was being divided between the tribes is the Bible's first instance of an appeal for equal rights for women. The power of their example is in their wisdom of trusting God to see that they were not denied. All five daughters manifested a balance between a spirit of confrontation and a spirit of cooperation. The former is illustrated by their attack on injustice and the latter by their compliance with the elder's decision that they should marry within their tribe. God defended them when they allowed Him to be their Deliverer and Provider. So shown in ancient history their actions reveal a contemporary pathway to overcoming inequality while sustaining a Godly spirit.

PHILLIP'S DAUGHTERS
Women and New Testament Ministry
Acts 21:9

This reference to Phillip's daughters exercising the gifts of prophecy makes clear that women did bring God's word by the power of the Holy Spirit and that such ministry was fully accepted in the early church. This is reinforced by Paul in 1 Cor. 11:5, where he directs 1) that a woman may prophesy, but 2) that she must be properly "covered", that is rightly related to her husband or other spiritual authority, a regulation incumbent upon all spiritual leaders- male or female. (1Tim 2:1-13)

It is puzzling why the place of women in ministry is contested by some in the church. Women had an equal place in the Upper Room, awaiting the Holy Spirit's coming and birth of the church (Act1:14). Then Peter's prophetic sermon at Pentecost affirmed the OT promise was now to be realized: "your daughters and maidservants would now share fully and equally with men in realizing the anointing, fullness, and ministry of the Holy Spirit, making them effective in witness and service for the spread of the gospel".

Though the place of men seems more pronounced in the numbers who filled leadership offices, there does not appear to be any direct restriction of privilege. The direct mention of Phoebe as a deacon (16:1) 2) John's letter to an elect chosen lady with instructions concerning whom she allows to minister in her house (2 John): and 3) where Chloe and Euodia seem to be women in whose homes believers gathered. The method of designation suggests they were the appointed leaders in their respective fellowships. 1Cor 1:11 and Phil 4:2,

The acceptance of women in a public place of ministry in the church is not a concession to the spirit of the feminist movement. Rather the refusal of such a place might be a concession to an order of male chauvinism, unwarranted by and unsupported in the scriptures. Clearly, women did speak, preach, and prophesy in the early church. (1Tim 2:6-15)

THE ANONYMOUS WOMAN
Mark 5:28

We don't know who she was, but we can empathize with her anxiety that day, and remember the lesson she taught us. It is one that's been told and retold millions of times over two thousand years, and it still astounds us today. The fact was, she dealt with an issue of blood for twelve years; had seen many doctors who were unable to help her. She heard that Jesus was in town, heard about His healing. With unshakable faith, she approached the crowd thinking," If I just touch the hem of His garment, I will be healed".

Oh, for the determined, undistracted, healing faith of that anonymous woman! Until Jesus spoke to her, she was a silent nobody in the crowd. But two thousand years later, the story of what she knew still speaks to us. She knew Jesus had the power to change her life for good. And I know, he still has that power today!

Chapter Four

UNDERSTANDING SPIRITUAL GIFTS

The Gifts of the Godhead

For many, clarification of the distinct role each member of the Godhead plays in giving gifts to mankind is helpful. Foundationally, of course, our existence, human life is given by the Father. (Gen 2:7; Heb. 12:9), who also gave His only begotten Son, as the Redeemer for mankind (John 3:16). Redemptively, Jesus has given eternal life. (John 5:38-40; 10:27, 28) He gave His life and shed His blood to gain that privilege (John 10:17, 18:Eph. 5:25-27). Further, the Father and Son have jointly sent the Holy Spirit (Acts 2:17, 33) to advance the work of redemption through the church's ministry of missions, growth, and evangelism. (Gen 2:7; Heb. 12:9) (John 3:16). (John 5:38-40; 10:27, 28) (John 10:17, 18:Eph. 5:25-27).

In the sequence, firstly, Romans 12:3-8 describes gifts given by God as Father. They seem to characterize basic motivations that are inherent tendencies that characterize each different person by reason of the Creator's unique workmanship in their initial gifting. While only seven categories are listed, observation indicates that few people are fully described by only one. More commonly a mix is found, with different traits of each gift present to some degree, while usually one will be the dominant trait of that person. It would be a mistake to suppose that an individual's learning to respond to the Creator's gifting of them in one or more of the categories fulfills the Bible call to earnestly desire the best gifts (1Cor. 12:31). These gifts of our place in God's created order are foundational.

Secondly, 1 Corinthians 12:7-11 lists the nine gifts of the Holy Spirit. Their purpose is specific to profit the body of the church. The word Profit is derived from a Greek word "sumphero" means to bring together, to benefit, to be advantageous," which is experienced as the body is strengthened in its life together and expanded through its ministry of evangelism. These nine gifts are available to every believer as the Holy Spirit distributes them (1Cor. 12:11). They are not to be merely acknowledged in a passive way, but rather are to be actively welcomed and expected (1Cor. 13:1; 14:1).

Thirdly, the gifts which the Son of God has given are pivotal in assuring that the first two categories of gifts are applied in the body of the church. Ephesians 4:7-16 not only indicates the *office gifts* Christ has placed in the church along with their purpose. The ministry of these leaders is to equip the body by assisting each person: 1) to perceive the place the Creator has made him to fill, by His creative workmanship in him and possibilities that salvation now opens to his realization of what he was made to be; and 2) to receive the power of the Holy Spirit, and begin to respond to His gifts, which are given to expand each believers capabilities beyond the created order and toward the redemptive dimension of ministry, for edifying the church and evangelizing the world.

In this light, we examine these clearly designated categories of gifting: the Father's (Rom. 12:6-8), the Son's (Eph. 4:11), and the Holy Spirit's (1 Cor. 12:8-10). While the study expands beyond those listings and the above outlined structure of the gifts of the Godhead, the general outline will help in two ways. Firstly, it assists us by noting the distinct interest and work of each member of the Trinity in providing for our unique purpose and fulfillment. Secondly, it prevents us from confusing our foundational motivation in life and service for God with our purposeful quest for and openness to His Holy Spirit's full resources and power for service and ministry.

Gifts of the Father (Basic Life Purpose and Motivation) Romans 12:3-8:

1. **Prophecy**
   a. To speak with forthrightness and insight, especially when enabled by the Spirit of God (Joel 2:28)
   b. To demonstrate moral boldness and uncompromising commitment to worthy values
   c. To influence others in one's arena of influence with a positive spirit of social or spiritual righteousness

2. **Ministry**
   a. To minister and render loving, general service that meet the needs of others
   b. To serve in the work and office of the deacon (Matt 20:26)

3. **Teaching**
   a. The supernatural ability to explain and apply the truths received from God for the church
   b. Presupposes study and the Spirit's illumination providing the ability to make divine truth clear to the people of God

c. Considered distinct from the work of the prophet who speaks as the direct mouthpiece of God

4. Exhortation
a. Literally means to call aside for the purpose of making an appeal
b. In a broader sense to entreat, comfort, or instruct (Acts 4:36; Heb 10:25)

5. Giving
a. To give out of a spirit of generosity
b. To bring resources to aid those without such resources (2 Cor. 8:2; 9:11-13)
c. Exercised without outward show or pride and with liberality (2Cor. 1:12; 8:2;,9:11, 13)

6. Leadership
a. Ability to provide guidance
b. Exercise of the Holy Spirit in modeling, superintending, and developing the body of Christ
c. Carried out with diligence
d. Acting with authority

7. Mercy
a. Sympathize with the misery of another
b. Relate to others in empathy, respect, and honesty
c. Practiced with kindness and cheerfulness-not as a matter of duty

Gifts of the Holy Spirit 1Corinthians 12:8-10, 28

1. Words of Wisdom
a. Supernatural, perspective to ascertain the divine means for accomplishing God's will in given situations.
b. Divinely given power to appropriate spiritual intuition in problem solving.

c. Being led by the Holy Spirit to act appropriately in a given set of circumstances.
Knowledge rightly applied with discernment

2. Word of Knowledge
a. Supernatural revelation of the divine will and plan.
b. Supernatural insight or understanding of circumstances without assistance of any human resource
c. Implies a deeper and more advanced understanding of the communicated acts of God
d. Involves moral wisdom for right living and relationships.
e. Requires objective understanding concerning divine things in human duties.
f. May also refer to knowledge of God or of the things that belong to God, as related in the gospel

3. Faith
a. Supernatural ability to believe God without doubt
b. Supernatural ability to meet adverse circumstances with trust in God's messages and words
c. Inner conviction impelled by an urgent and higher calling

4. Gifts of Healing
a. Refers to supernatural healing without human aid.
b. May include divinely assisted application of human instrumentation and medical means of treatment.
c. Does not discount the use of God's creative gifts.

5. Working of Miracles
a. Supernatural power to intervene and counteract earthly and evil forces.
b.   a display of power giving the ability to go beyond the natural.

c. Operates closely with the gifts of faith and healing to bring authority over sin, Satan, sickness, and the binding forces of this age

6. Prophecy
a. Divinely inspired and anointed utterance
b. Supernatural proclamation in a known language
c. Manifestation of the Spirit of God-not of intellect(1 Cor. 12:7) calling forth words from the Spirit of God
d. possessed and operated by all who have the infilling of the Holy Spirit (1Cor.14:31)

7. Discerning of Spirits
a. Supernatural power to detect the realm of the spirit and their activities.
b. Implies the power of spiritual insight for revelation of plans and purposes of the Enemy and his forces

8. Speaking in Tongues
a. Supernatural utterance in languages not known to the speaker; a means of communication inspired by the Holy Spirit
b. Serves as an evidence and sign of indwelling and working of the Holy Spirit.

9. Interpretation of Tongues
a. Supernatural power to reveal the meaning of tongue.
b. Functions not as the operation as the mind of man but of the spirit
c. Interpreter does not serve as a translation, but rather is a declaration of meaning
d. Is exercised as a miraculous and supernatural phenomenon as are the gift of speaking in tongues and the gift of prophecy.
Ephesians 4:11 (Also 1Cor. 12:28):

Gifts of the Son (Facilitate and Equip the Body of the Church) Ephesians 4:11 1Cor. 12:28):

1. **Apostles**
   a. In apostolic days referred to a select group chosen to carry out directly the ministry of Christ; included the assigned task given to a few to complete the sacred canon of the Holy Scriptures.
   b. Implies the exercise of a distinct representative role of broader leadership given by Christ.
   c. Functions as a messenger or spokesman of God.
   d. In contemporary times refers to those who have the spirit of apostleship in extending the work of the church, opening fields to the gospel, and overseeing larger sections of the body of Jesus Christ.

2. **Prophet**
   a. A spiritually mature spokesman/ proclaimer with a special, divinely focused message to the church or the world
   b. A person uniquely gifted at times with insight into future events

3. **Evangelist**
   a. Refers primarily to a special gift of preaching or witnessing in a way that brings unbelievers into the experience of salvation
   b. Functionally, the gift of evangelist operates for the establishment of new works, while pastors and teachers follow up to organize and sustain
   c. operates to establish converts and to gather them spiritually and literally into the body of Christ

4. Pastor/ Teacher
a. The word *pastor* comes from a root word meaning to protect from which we get the word shepherd.
b. Implies the function of a shepherd/leader to nurture, teach, and care for the spiritual needs of the body.

5. Missionary
(Some refer to apostle or evangelist)
a. Implies the unfolding of a plan for making the gospel known to all the world (Rom. 1:16)
b. Illustrates an attitude of humility for receiving a call to remote areas and unknown situations
(Is. 6:1-13)
c. Connotes an inner compulsion to lead the whole world to an understanding of Jesus Christ(2Cor. 5:14-20)
d.

Special Graces

1. Hospitality
a. Means to love and do with pleasure and sincerity.
b. Teaching and practical service (1Peter 4:10, 11).
c. Utilized in caring for believers and workers who visit to worship, work, and become apart of the body of Christ.
d. Illustrated in the teaching of Jesus concerning judgment (Matt. 25:35, 40)

2. Celibacy
(Matt 19:10: 1 Cor.7:7-9, 27; 1Tim. 4:3; Rev. 14:4)

a. The Bible considers marriage to be honorable, ordained of God, and a need for every person.
b. Implies a special gift which frees the individual from the duties, pressures, and preoccupations of family life, thereby, allowing undivided attention to the Lord's work.

3. Martyrdom

a. Illustrated in the spirit of Stephen (Acts 7:59, 60)
b. Fulfilled in the attitude of Paul (2Tim. 4:6-8)

Things to Ponder
SPIRITUAL GIFTS

1. **What thoughts and images come to mind when you think of the spiritual gifts?**

2. **Discuss what you believe is the best definition for the term spiritual gifts.**

3. **Discuss how the following verses relate to spiritual gifts. Look in a fresh way at each passage, searching especially for (a) God's commands and standards to keep, (b) someone's example to learn from, (c) a promise from God to believe, (d) a warning to heed, or (e) a challenge to face.**

- John 16:13-15
- Rom 12:6-8
- 1 Cor. 12; 14
- Gal 5:22
- Eph 4:11
- 2 Tim 1:6-7
- 1 Peter 4:11

4. What vital, fundamental principles can you see in these passages?

5. Finally, answer these questions, especially in light of what you have observed in the passages above: (a) what does God want me to understand most about Himself? (b) What does God want me to understand most about others? (c) What does God want me to understand most about myself? And in light of all this, what would He have me do?

Chapter Five

UNDERSTANDING SPIRITUAL AUTHORITY

AUTHORITY

The power or right to do something particularly to give orders and see that they are followed. The word authority as used in the Bible usually means a person's right to do certain things because of the position or office he holds. This word emphasizes the legality and right, more than the physical strength, needed to do something.

The two basic forms of authority are intrinsic authority (belonging to one's essential nature) and derived authority (given to one from another source). Since "there is no authority except from God" (Rom 13:1), every kind of authority other than that of God Himself is derived and therefore secondary to God's power (John 19:11).

God's authority is absolute and unconditional (Ps 29:10; Isa 40:1). He has authority over nature (Job 38), governments (Dan 4:17, 34-35), and history (Acts 1:7; 17:24-31); and He has the power to send people to hell (Luke 12:5). Jesus Christ has the same intrinsic authority as the Father (John 10:25-30), although this authority is said to be given to Christ from His Father, just as the authority of the Holy Spirit is given to Him from the Father and the Son (John

14:26; 15:26; 16:13-15). Christ has the authority to forgive sins (John 5:26-27), to lay down His life and take it up again (John 10:17-18), and to give eternal life (John 17:2). The people were astonished at this authority which Jesus revealed when He taught and performed miracles (Matt 7:28-29; 8:27; Luke 4:36).

In addition to the intrinsic authority of God, the Bible speaks of many kinds of derived power. Some of the most important of these are the authority of civil governments (Rom 13:1-7), parents (Eph 6:1-4), employers (Eph 6:5-9), church leaders (Heb 13:7, 17), angels (Luke 1:19-20), Satan (Luke 4:6), and evil spirits other than Satan (Eph 6:11-12). There are vast differences among these kinds of authority. Some are permitted by God only for a time.

One derived authority is above every other kind of derived authority, and that is the Bible. Because the Bible is inspired by God (2 Tim 3:16; 2 Peter 1:20-21), it has divine power and authority. God did not give the Scriptures to be read only, but to be believed and obeyed.

Christians are often given certain authority to exercise. This includes the authority of a parent or a church leader. The noblest use of authority is for serving others. "Let...he who governs," Jesus said, be "as he who serves....I am among you as the One who serves" (Luke 22:26-27). The Christian who seeks to follow Christ's example will learn to use authority with others more than over others. The wise Christian remembers that all derived authority will one day be returned to the God who gave it (1 Cor. 15:24-28). But the rewards of faithful service will endure throughout eternity (1 John 2:17).

POWER

Power is the ability or strength to perform an activity or deed. Power is sometimes used with the word authority. If power suggests physical strength, authority suggests a moral right or privilege. One can have power to perform a task but not authority to do it. Jesus Christ had both power and authority (Luke 4:36), and He bestowed these upon His followers (Luke 10:19).

Submission to Spiritual Authority

Biblical submission is an act of the will demonstrated by serving others out of an attitude that regards them as more important than yourself.

Biblical Submission is not slavery. It is a very fundamental principle of life that is to be practiced in the church and the world. There are many emphatic scriptures on how spiritual authority should govern and guide the church as well as instructions about the right response to authority, both civil and spiritual. The bible is very clear on the subject of submission not just in the church but also for husbands, wives, children, and employees, civil, parental and spiritual authority.

Understand the principle of submission and you'll understand the practice of submission. Submission to spiritual authority is about a functional relationship of love and honor to God first, then to man.

As I read the scriptures I see a couple of words in the Bible that are synonymous with submission; Honor, respect, giving, love and humility

Find a person who understands submission to authority and you'll see a person who is humble, full of love, unselfish, accountable, and personally responsible.

Find a person who does not understand submission to authority and you'll see a person who is prideful, full of criticism, selfish, self ruled, and spiritually irresponsible.

WARNING: Beware of people who are always finding fault with the leadership of the church and the church itself. With this divisive spirit clothing, their hearts are rebellious and their fruit is pride and dishonor. They seek to destroy people, the church and even the faith while lifting up themselves and their cause. They are bitter against leaders and long for control. Watch out for them for they claim to love God and His commands but yet rejected His delegated authority.

Let's go to the scriptures about submission to spiritual authority:

Ephesians 4:11 And he gave some, apostles; and some, prophets; and some, evangelists; and some, pastors and teachers; 12 For the perfecting of the saints, for the work of the ministry, for the edifying of the body of Christ:
Jesus is head of the church and He has established these offices as well as people to be leaders with authority in those offices over the church. God also has given these leaders the responsibility to serve, oversee, and establish HIS word and

commands for HIS church in the earth. See also Eph 5:20-28; 6:1; Col 3:20.

Hebrews 13:17 Obey them that have the rule over you, and submit yourselves: for they watch for your souls, as they that must give account, that they may do it with joy, and not with grief: for that is unprofitable for you. 18 Pray for us: for we trust we have a good conscience, in all things willing to live honestly. Clearly this is not talking about civil authorities, but spiritual authority. It says OBEY and SUBMIT. (Swear words to some Christians). But Paul also said, PRAY for spiritual leaders.

Look at these two scriptures about honoring spiritual leaders.

1 Tim. 5:17 Let the elders that rule well be counted worthy of double honour, especially they who labour in the word and doctrine.

1 Thess. 5:12 and we beseech you, brethren, to know them which labour among you, and are over you in the Lord, and admonish you; 13 And to esteem them very highly in love for their work's sake. And be at peace among yourselves.

More than ruling over people, spiritual leaders have an obligation to Jesus Christ to love, feed, and protect the flock of God. God has given them His grace and authority to govern. Along with that responsibility come instruction, counsel, warning, correction, and even rebuke when necessary. Spiritual authority or leadership is more than a title; it is a relationship with people. They stand as servants, ministers, and even spiritual parents in the lives of God's people. Read 1 Cor. 4:14-16.

In many instances Paul gave commands to the church and even put people out of the church for disobedience and sin.

In fact one time Paul said that the leaders of the church were to turn someone over to Satan that they learn not to blaspheme. Read 2Thessolonian 3:10-14.

Leaders are to be a strong godly example and to lead in strength and certainty. However, many people are offended by this quality and cry "spiritual abuse". They are simply offended at God's word rather than the leader.

The principles of submission are submitting in the fear of God and as unto the Lord and loving and giving as Jesus did. Submission isn't a power struggle but rather a mutual relationship of love, humility, and respect. It is a principle that should be practiced in every area of life, including the church, for it is godly order and divine principles for safety and success.

AGAIN; Understand the principle of submission and you'll understand the practice of submission

 The real love of Jesus is expressed through submission Christians we are commanded to LOVE and SERVE one another. (Gal. 5:13)

Civil Authority – Scriptural Basis

Rom. 13:1 Let every soul be subject unto the higher powers. For there is no power but of God: the powers that be are ordained of God. 2 Whosoever therefore resisteth the power resisteth the ordinance of God: and they that resist shall receive to themselves damnation. 3 For rulers are not a terror to good works, but to the evil. Wilt thou then not be afraid of the power? Do that which is good and thou shalt have praise of the same: 4 For he is the minister of God to thee for good. But if thou do that which is evil, be afraid; for he beareth not the sword in vain: for he is the minister of God, a revenger to execute wrath upon him that doeth evil.

The correlation between governmental authority or *non-spiritual* authority and God's authority is very clear. God has not only established authority among men but, honors their judgment and punishment. The higher powers or rulers are called Ministers of God, first the natural then the spiritual.

NOTICE: Only those breaking the law have an issue with the law! The same as in the church only those who hate authority will not submit to authority. But those who understand the principle of authority understand the practice of submission.

Submission is about being a servant out of love for God and others. Jesus constantly admonished the disciples to be servants and to lay their life down for the Gospels sake instead of being concerned about ruling over people. Jesus submitted to his parents and He was subject to those over Him. Jesus increased in wisdom and stature and in favor with God and man by being under authority and therefore being answerable for His character. Submission is a position you take and then a condition you live.

Jesus not only showed us submission to natural authorities but He also demonstrated submission to spiritual authority when he said, "I can of mine own self do nothing: as I hear, I judge: and my judgment is just; because I seek not mine own will, but the will of the Father which hath sent me." (John 5:30)

This is sage advice for Christians to submit to spiritual and as well as civil authority.

The Benefits of Spiritual Authority

Spiritual authority may not be a very popular topic among Christians as society has impacted our lives in ways that deter this principle. An underlying factor is it is given to you. Never assumed! However, when one operates under spiritual authority, you gain access with unlimited power in the supernatural and nothing is impossible. Understand how following spiritual authority will yield miracles, blessings, in marriage and home, and receive prosperity.

The fact is that you are either under authority of God or in rebellion against God! Jesus says in His Word, "He that is not for Me is against Me!"

Yes, you can be a silent rebel! It does not matter if you are a Bible toting, scripture quoting rebel, you are still a rebel following the ultimate rebel, Satan, who rebelled against God and is the prince of rebels.

First of all, Christians must acknowledge one of the fundamentals of spiritual authority, which is that spiritual authority is given to you, it is never assumed!

For example, if you are in the military, your authority is earned and given to you. You do not finish boot camp and assume you are General Petraeus. The road to rank is marked by years of faithful service and accomplishment.

Similarly, in the Kingdom of God, you do not get saved and 12 weeks later try to be Billy Graham. You are to find a place of service, get under spiritual authority and accomplish something by producing good fruit.

Only then will you be in a position to be in spiritual authority.

The point is that it takes time to produce good fruit. America is full of church bunnies that are hopping from church to church. Then, forty years later they are still "Privates" in the Kingdom of God as opposed to the five star Generals they should be. They have not been under spiritual authority and they have not produced any fruit. Instead, they have confused motion with progress and accomplish absolutely nothing!

Furthermore, the Word of God says that if you rebel against spiritual authority you will bring the judgment of God on yourself. Romans 13:2 read, *"Therefore whoever resists the authority of God will bring judgment on yourself!"*

Have you ever considered that when you speak against spiritual authority you are speaking against God who set that spiritual authority? Christians must realize that if we reject God's authority, then God will reject us. In John 13:20 Jesus said, *"Most assuredly, I say to you, He who receives whomever I send receives Me and he who receives Me receives Him who sent Me."*

Another principle of spiritual authority this sermon series will teach you is the concept that the spiritual world controls the physical world.

Consider this: Adam and Eve had a perfect existence in the Garden of Eden until they sinned and rebelled against God's authority. Their submission to God's authority totally controlled what happened in the physical world. When they sinned, their spiritual relationship with God was severed and their curse immediately followed.

Conversely, one needs look no further than Daniel to see the reward for those who follow spiritual authority. He was thrown in the lion's den because he refused to disobey his spiritual authority. Although the lions had been starved to guarantee Daniel would be ripped to shreds, Daniel prayed, and the spiritual world controlled the physical world as angels muzzled the mouths of those hungry lions and Daniel was saved.

In addition to this, this sermon series will also show you the correlation between spiritual authority and financial prosperity. Just like God controls the spiritual world, He also controls the financial world. The Word of God says, "All the gold and the silver are mine said the Lord!" And "It is the Lord that gives you the power to get wealth!"

Some people are confused by this concept. They ask, "Doesn't the Bible say Jesus became poor?" Yes, it does! But the question is this, when, where and why did He become poor? Christ became poor at the Cross for our sake! So that we might exchange our poverty for His riches, become heirs and joint heirs with Jesus Christ and that we might have the favor and blessings of Abraham here and in eternity!

So, if you have to follow spiritual authority in order to reap financial blessings, what is the first principle the Bible commands for financial success? Tithing! So, why do we tithe? We tithe because God the Father commands us to do it and refusal to tithe is a rebellion against the Word of God, the will of God, and the authority of God.

The Word of God says in Malachi 3:10, *"Bring ye all the tithes into the storehouse..."*Notice it does not request "some" of the tithe, it demands "all" of the tithe. So, are you giving God what is right? Or, are you giving Him what is left?

The Word commands you tithe 10% of your income. You are not giving to God 10% of what is yours, you are merely giving Him 10% of what he has blessed you with—it was already His in the first place. Leviticus 27:30 says, *"All the tithe of the land, whether of the seed of the land or of the fruit of the tree, is the Lord's."*

When you follow spiritual authority and tithe as you are commanded to do, then God will give you an increase of income. Malachi 3:10 says, *"Prove Me now said the Lord of Hosts... If I will not open the windows of heaven and pour out on you blessings that there will not be room enough to receive."* The point is that you do not pray and ask in order to receive financial blessings; you tithe in order to receive them. But God will not give you more until you are faithful to give what you already have!

So, would you like to have so much prosperity you had trouble figuring out what to do with your wealth? Then tithe! Thinking you can gain wealth by investing in things that will eventually be lost is foolish and irresponsible. The Word reminds us that, "Heaven and earth shall pass away..." So, the day will come when all you will have left is what you have given to God in this life.

These concepts are just a glimpse of what this sermon series has in store for you. I urge you to listen to this message and learn how to begin reaping the benefits of spiritual authority in your finances, your marriage, and your life today!

Things to Ponder
LEADERSHIP

1.   Discuss what you believe is the best definition for the word leadership. What exactly does a leader do?

2.   What qualities impress you most in a good leader? What qualities lease impressive in a leader?

3.   Read the following verses related to leadership. Take a fresh look at each passage, searching especially for (a) God's commands and standards to keep, (b) examples to learn and follow, (c) promises from God to believe, (d) warnings to heed, or (e) challenges to face.

   ·   Ex 18:•24-26
   ·   Josh 1
   ·   1 Sam 18:16
   ·   Ps 78:70-72
   ·   Prov. 16:10; 20:8, 26, 28; 22:11; 28:3, 15-16; 29:4
   ·   Luke 22:24-30
   ·   1 Tim 3:1-13; 4:11-12

4.   What vital, fundamental principles can you see in these passages (principles which are consistent with other Scriptures you know)?

5. What vital, fundamental principles can you see in these passages, especially in light of what you have observed: What does God want me to understand most about Himself, myself, and others? In light of all this, what would He have me do?

UNDERSTANDING SPRITUAL WARFARE

Ephesians 2:1-6, "And you hath he quickened, who were dead in trespasses and sins; wherein in time past ye walked according to the course of this world, according to the prince of the power of the air, the spirit that now worketh in the children of disobedience: among whom also we all had our conversation in times past in the lusts of our flesh, fulfilling the desires of the flesh and of the mind; and were by nature the children of wrath, even as others. But God, who is rich in mercy, for his great love wherewith he loved us, even when we were dead in sins, hath quickened us together with Christ, (by grace ye are saved); and hath raised us up together, and made us sit together in heavenly place in Christ Jesus."

Prior to our conversion into the family of God, we were all dead in our trespasses and sins. However, now that we are saved, we have a (1) Position in the family of God; (2) Position with Christ; and a (3) Position in heavenly places. Colossians 1:13, says it this way, "Who hath delivered us from the power of darkness, and hath translated us into the Kingdom of his dear Son." Clearly, this scripture alone indicates that there are two forces (Kingdoms) warring against each other – the kingdom of God and the Kingdom of the Devil.

Much of Jesus' earthly ministry was spent casting out devils and modeling principles of Spiritual Warfare. Since we are followers of Christ and Satan did not like Jesus, consequently, he is an enemy of the saints also. THEREFORE, SAINTS, WE ARE IN A WAR! But rest assured we win and Satan is already a defeated foe. Our big brother, Jesus, declared our victory over 2000 years ago. "And having spoiled principalities and powers, he made a show of them openly, triumphing over them in it" (Colossians 2:15). Also, remember we are not fighting for the victory, but we are fighting from a victory platform (II Corinthians 2:14). It is Satan's job to discourage the saints and make them think they are defeated, but in reality he is defeated.

When we speak about spiritual warfare know that basically, there are two divisions of spiritual Warfare. One division deals strictly with casting out devils (commonly known as the Deliverance Ministry), and the second division deals with warfare against the different ranks of Satan's army (Ephesians 6:10-12). This manual will be dealing primarily with the latter.

Just as God has an organized army so does Satan. What saints must recognize is that we are not on a playground with Satan, but rather, we are on a battleground. Revelation 13:7 says, "And it was given unto him to make war with the saints and to overcome them..." As Christian soldiers we must be thoroughly furnished and equipped to fight the battle. "Lest Satan should get an advantage of us: for we are not ignorant of his devices" (II Corinthians 2:11). "And from the days of John the Baptist until now the Kingdom of heaven suffereth violence, and the violent take it by force" (Matthew 11:12).

COMMON ATTACK AREAS

1. Your Mind

II Corinthians 11:3, "But I fear, lest by any means, as the serpent beguiled Eve through his subtilty, so your minds should be corrupted from the simplicity that is in Christ."

> A. Lies (Revelation 12:9, Romans 1:25, II Corinthians 11:13-14, Galatians 1:8, I Timothy 4:1-2)
>
> John 8:44, "Ye are of your father, the devil, and the lusts of your father ye will do. He was a murderer from the beginning, and abode not in the truth, because there is no truth in him. When he speaketh a lie, he speaketh of his own: for he is a liar, and the father of it."

> B. Accuser (Zechariah 3:1-4, NIV)
>
> Revelation 12:10, "And I heard a loud voice saying in heaven, Now is come salvation, and strength, and the kingdom of our God, and the power of his Christ: for the accuser of our brethren is cast down, which accused them before our God day and night."

2. Your Body

I Peter 5:8, "Be sober, be vigilant; because your adversary the devil, as a roaring lion, walketh about, seeking whom he may devour."

> If Satan cannot defeat you in your mind, then he will attack your body with afflictions and diseases.

"And ought not this woman, being a daughter of Abraham, whom Satan hath bound, lo, these eighteen years, be loosed from this bond on the sabbath day?" Luke 13:16

Satan's desire is to cause suffering and shame to the child of God. If he can effectively do this, then he can bring shame to the Word of God.

WARRING A GOOD WARFARE

"This charge I commit unto thee, son Timothy, according to the prophecies whichwent before on thee, that thou by them mightest war a good warfare."

I Timothy 1:18

In order for saints to war a good warfare, there are several things they must know and understand.

1. Saints must recognize the <u>power</u> and the <u>authority</u> that has been invested in the name of Jesus.

Ephesians 1:20-22, "Which he wrought in Christ, when he raised him from the dead, and set him at his own right hand in the heavenly places, Far above all principality, and power, and might, and dominion, and every name that is named, not only in this world, but also in that which is to come: And hath put all things under his feet, and gave him to be the head over all things to the church."

2. Jesus has delegated this authority and power to the believers.

Luke 10:19, "Behold, I give unto you power to tread on serpents and scorpions, and over all the power of the enemy: and nothing shall by any means hurt you."

3. You need to be filled with the Holy Spirit.

Acts 1:8, "But ye shall receive power, after that the Holy Ghost is come upon you: and ye shall be witnesses unto me both in Jerusalem, and in all Judaea, and in Samaria, and unto the uttermost part of the earth."

4. We must have faith and patience to receive the promises
of God.

Hebrews 6:12, "That ye be not slothful, but followers of them who through faith and patience inherit the promises."

5. Must be properly dressed.

[10] Finally, my brethren, be strong in the Lord, and in the power of his might.

[11] Put on the whole armour of God, that ye may be able to stand against the wiles of the devil.

[12] For we wrestle not against flesh and blood, but against principalities, against powers, against the rulers of the darkness of this world, against spiritual wickedness in high places.

[13] **Wherefore take unto you the whole armour of God,** that ye may be able to withstand in the evil day, and having done all, to stand.

[14] Stand therefore, having <u>your loins girt about with truth,</u> and having on <u>the breastplate of righteousness;</u>

[15] <u>And your feet shod with the preparation of the gospel of peace;</u>

[16] Above all, taking <u>the shield of faith,</u> wherewith ye shall be able to quench all the fiery darts of the wicked.

[17] And take <u>the helmet of salvation,</u> and <u>the sword of the Spirit, which is the word of God:</u>

Ephesian 6:10-17

Chapter Seven

UNDERSTANDING THE POWER OF PRAYER

PRAYER

Introduction

Today's dilemma, I believe stems from a lack of prayer by believers. God has given dominion and authority to the born again, blood washed, Holy Ghost filled believer (blood bought). There are not enough believers who agree with God therefore it seems the enemy is waging war and winning.

Prayer is communication between God and the believer which consists of petitions, supplications, thanksgiving and intercessions to God by the believer to align his or her will with the Word of God. (Ephesians 2:6) The three together note our union with Christ in His resurrection, His ascension, and in His present rule at God's right hand. He is sitting at the right hand of the Father making intercessions on our behalf. From the place of partnership, he grants that we share in the present works of His kingdom's power by prayer.

Prayer is conversing with God; the intercourse of the soul with God, not in contemplation or meditation, but in direct address to him. Prayer may be oral or mental, occasional or constant, ejaculatory or formal. It is a *beseeching the Lord* (Ex 32:11); *pouring out the soul before the Lord* (1 Sam 1:15); *praying and crying to heaven* (2 Chron. 32:20); *seeking unto God and making supplication* (Job 8:5); *drawing near to God* (Ps 73:28); *bending the knees* (Eph 3:14).

Prayer presupposes a belief in the personality of God, His ability and willingness to hold intercourse with us, His personal control of all things, all of his creatures and all of their actions. God is personal and all people can offer prayers; however, sinners who have not trusted Jesus Christ for their salvation remain alienated from God. While unbelievers may pray, they do not have the basis for a rewarding fellowship with God. They have not met the conditions laid down in the Bible for effectiveness in prayer.

Prayer cannot be replaced by devout good works in a needy world. Important as service to others is, at times we must turn away from it to God, who is distinct from all things and over all things. Neither should prayer be thought of as a mystical experience in which people lose their identity in the infinite reality. Effective prayer must be a scripturally informed response of persons saved by grace to the living God who can hear and answer on the basis of Christ's payment of the penalty which sinners deserved.

Christians recognize their dependence upon their Creator. They have every reason to express gratitude for God's blessings. But they have far more reason to respond to God than this. They respond to the love of God for them. God's love is revealed through the marvelous incarnation and life of Christ, His atoning provision at the Cross, His resurrection, as well as His continuing presence through the Holy Spirit. Prayer involves these important aspects:

1. Faith. The most meaningful prayer comes from a heart that places its trust in the God who has acted and spoken in the Jesus of history and the teachings of the Bible. God speaks to us through the Bible, and we in turn speak to Him in trustful, believing prayer. Assured by the Scripture that God is personal, living, active, all-knowing, all-wise, and all-powerful, we know that God can hear and help us. A confident prayer life is built on the cornerstone of Christ's work and words as shown by the prophets and apostles in the Spirit-inspired writings of the Bible.

2. Worship. In worship we recognize what is of highest worth-not ourselves, others, or our work, but God. Only the highest divine being deserves our highest respect. Guided by Scripture, we set our values in accord with God's will and perfect standards. Before God, angels hide their faces and cry, "Holy, holy, holy is the Lord of hosts" (Isa 6:3).

3. Confession. Awareness of God's holiness leads to consciousness of our own sinfulness. Like the prophet Isaiah, we exclaim, "Woe is me, for I am undone! Because I am a man of unclean lips, and I dwell in the midst of a people of unclean lips; for my eyes have seen the King, the Lord of hosts" (Isa 6:5). By sinning we hurt ourselves and those closest to us; but first and worst of all, sin is against God (Ps 51:4). We must confess our sins directly to God rather than to another human being for He promises to forgive us of all our unrighteousness (1 John 1:9).

4. Adoration. God is love, and He has demonstrated His love in the gift of His Son (John 3:16). The greatest desire of God is that we love Him with our whole being (Matt 22:37). Our love should be expressed as His has been expressed, in both deeds and words. People sometimes find it difficult to say to others and to God, "I love you." But when love for God fills our lives, we will express our love in prayer to the one who is ultimately responsible for all that we are.

5. Praise. The natural outgrowth of faith, worship, confession, and adoration is praise. We speak well of one whom we highly esteem and love. The one whom we respect and love above all others naturally receives our highest commendation. We praise Him for His "mighty acts...according to His excellent greatness!" (Ps 150:2), and for His "righteous judgments" (Ps 119:164). For God Himself, for His works, and for His words, His people give sincere praise.

6. Thanksgiving. Are we unthankful because we think we have not received what we deserve? But if we got what we "deserved," we would be condemned because of our guilt. As sinners, we are not people of God by nature. We have no claim upon His mercy or grace. Nevertheless, He has forgiven our sins, granted us acceptance as His people, and given us His righteous standing and a new heart and life. Ingratitude marks the ungodly (Rom 1:21). Believers, in contrast, live thankfully. God has been at work on our behalf in countless ways. So in everything, even for the discipline that is unpleasant, we give thanks (Col 3:17; 1 Thess. 5:18).

7. Dedicated Action. Christ's example does not require us to withdraw from society, but to render service to the needy in a spirit of prayer. He wept over Jerusalem in compassionate prayer, and then He went into the city to give His life a ransom for many. Authentic prayer will be the source of courage and productivity, as it was for the prophets and apostles.

8. Request. Prayer is not only response to God's grace as brought to us in the life and work of Jesus and the teaching of Scripture; it is also request for our needs and the needs of others.

God has promised to answer our requests when we:

1. help the hungry and afflicted (Isa 58:9-10),
2. believe that we will receive what we ask (Mark 11:22-24),
3. forgive others (Mark 11:25-26),
4. ask in Christ's name (John 14:13-14),
5. abide in Christ and His words (John 15:7),
6. pray in the Spirit (Eph 6:8), obey the Lord's commandments (1 John 3:22), and
7. Ask according to His will (1 John 5:14-15).

For good reasons God's holy and wise purpose does not permit Him to grant every petition just as it is asked.
Hindrances to answered prayer are mentioned in the bible;

1. iniquity in the heart (Ps 66:18),
2. refusal to hear God's law (Prov. 28:9),
3. an estranged heart (Isa 29:13),
4. sinful separation from God (Isa 59:2),
5. waywardness (Jer. 14:10-12),
6. offering unworthy sacrifices (Mal 1:7-9),
7. praying to be seen of men (Matt 6:5-6),

8. pride in fasting and tithing (Luke 18:11-14),
9. lack of faith (Heb 11:6),
10. doubting or double-mindedness (James 4:3).

Biblical responses to prayer:

1.   "Abraham's servant prayed to God, and God directed him to the person who should be wife to his Master's son and heir (Gen 24:10-20).
2. "Jacob prayed to God, and God inclined the heart of his irritated brother, so that they met in peace and friendship (Gen 32:24-30; 33:1-4).
3. "Samson prayed to God, and God showed him a well where he quenched his burning thirst and so lived to judge Israel (Judg. 15:18-20).
4. "David prayed, and God defeated the counsel of Ahithophel (2 Sam 15:31; 16:20-23; 17:14-23).
5. "Daniel prayed, and God enabled him both to tell Nebuchadnezzar his dream and to give the interpretation of it (Dan 2:16-23).
6. "Nehemiah prayed, and God inclined the heart of the king of Persia to grant him leave of absence to visit and rebuild Jerusalem (Neh. 1:11; 2:1-6).
7."Esther and Mordecai prayed, and God defeated the purpose of Haman, and saved the Jews from destruction (Est. 4:15-17; 6:7, 8).
8. "The believers in Jerusalem prayed, and God opened the prison doors and set Peter at liberty, when Herod had resolved upon his death (Acts 12:1-12).
9."Paul prayed that the thorn in the flesh might be removed, and his prayer brought a large increase of spiritual strength, while the thorn perhaps remained (2 Cor. 12:7-10).

I. Principles Governing Warfare (Deut 20, Ephes. 6)

1. Your authority must be demonstrated and established through prayer.
In Ephesians 2:6, the three together note our union with Christ 1) in his resurrection 2) his ascension
3) And in His present rule at Gods right hand. From the place of partnership,He grants that we share in the present works of His kingdoms power by prayer. (He is sitting at the right hand of the Father making intercessions on our behalf)

2. You must have forgiveness in Prayer
Mark 11:25-26, 25 "And whenever you stand praying, if you have anything against anyone, forgive him,
That your Father in heaven may also forgive you your trespasses. 26 But if you do not forgive,Neither will your Father in heaven forgive your trespasses."

3. You cannot base your faith prayers on your natural five physical senses. Your receiving happens when you pray in the spirit, not what you see, feel, smell, and hear in the natural.
Mark 11:24, therefore I say to you, whatever things you ask when you pray, believe that you receive them, and you will have them.

4. When you pray is your receiving day; When the presence of God comes, you must repeat what you received in prayer.

5. Prayer is the key to discerning our adversaries' strategies. Through prayer God will reveal the strategies of the enemy. (2Kings 6)

II. Realizing Our Power in Prayer James 5:15-16

John Wesley says it seems as though God only responds when people pray. God is not ruling and reigning in this world, only in the lives of those who have submitted to him and prayer. (2 Chron. 7:14, Luke 18:1, Ephes. 6:17-18),

AS A BELIEVER WE ARE GOD'S AMBASSADORS ON EARTH (2 Cor. 5:20-21), **YOU MUST**:

1) **Believe you receive when you pray.**
   Mark 11:24 "Therefore I say to you, whatever things you ask when you pray, believe that you receive them and you will have them"

2) **Pray in the Name of Jesus.**
   "And in that day you will ask Me nothing. Most assuredly, I say to you, whatever you ask the Father in My name He will give you. Until now you have asked nothing in My name. Ask, and you will receive, that your joy may be full.
   John 16:23-24

3) **Pray with authority.** The name of Jesus is your badge of authority Phil 2:9-11, Eph 1:19-23
   Therefore God also has highly exalted Him and given Him the name which is above every name, 10 that at the name of Jesus every knee should bow, of those in heaven, and of those on earth, and of those under the earth, 11 and that every tongue should confess that Jesus Christ is Lord, to the glory of God the Father.

4) Pray the Word 1Thess 5: 16-19

5) Pray without ceasing Matt 16:19-20; 18:18-20, Luke 7: 6-17)

III. When we fail to PRAY, We become PREY for the enemy.

Gen 49:27, Benjamin- the beloved of the Lord is a ravenous wolf: Why? Because in the morning, he shall devour the prey and at night he shall divide the spoil only if he prays.

The enemy seeks those whom he can devour *(1Peter 5:8)* **When God becomes your God, you will no longer be a prey for the enemy.** (Ezekiel 34: 20-31)

What is Prey?
1. Prey means- spoil, booty
2. Animals taken by a predator as food
3. One that is helpless or unable to resist attack; victim
4. To seize and devour (See Deut 8)
5. To commit violence or robbery or fraud
6. To have injuries, destructive, or wasting effect.

You become prey when;
- You don't depart from evil. (Ezekiel 34:8)
- You do not consistently pray
- You are not planted in the house of prayer (Luke 19:46)
- Sin is in your life and you have an unrepentant attitude

You are the enemy's enemy which becomes your prey through prayer. The enemy will perish for lack of prey.

Reflect on this Prayer:

Lord, help me to keep a prayerful attitude about everything. Remind me Holy Spirit of the importance and the power of prayer at all times. Don't let me become weary and distressed. When my heart is overwhelmed lead me to the rock that is higher than I. Help me to rely upon and have total confidence in You with every detail in my life. Help me to know that through prayer, I can counteract the enemy's onslaughts set against me. Help me to know that I need you every second, minute, and hour. You are my God and through prayer to You, I shall devour my enemies. Help me to control my emotions, my fears and control my concerns knowing that all things work together for my good.

I don't know the challenges that I will face from day to day. Be my anchor. Don't let them overtake me. Help me to know that you allowed it so it is making me greater in you. Help me to trust you completely. Help me to stand boldly when facing opposition. In the Name of Jesus. AMEN

Separation from God: Uniting with God through Prayer

Have you ever felt like God wasn't with you or that He wasn't hearing your prayers? When you pray do you feel a void and you can't get a prayer through? Or you need God to move for you and it seems as though He is so far from you? You feel forsaken or left abandoned by God. You have no place. (Example; Adam & eve, Jesus on the cross)

Such situations do exist, but they are not insurmountable for our iniquities (those in the heart which cannot be seen) have separated us from God and our sins (outward disobedience to God's word) have hidden His face from you according to Isaiah 59: 1-29.

In order to repair this breach, Intercession is essential.

What is Intercession?
Intercession is to reach God; to meet God; to pressure; to entreat; to urge God strongly; to encounter; to assail with urgent petitions for favor.

Intercession means to stand in the gap. Standing in the gap is a metaphor for committed intercession. There is a gap between God and man that an intercessor tries to repair.

To meet up with the enemy with hostile intent; the idea being a supplicant; Catching up with a superior and reaches him with an urgent request.

Role of an intercessor

The intercessor always comes before God on behalf of others.
Intercessors place the ministry of prayer with the word as highest in importance.

Intercessors links God's mercy with human need.

Intercessors are faithful in prayer and spiritual warfare. **Prayer has to be continuous because spiritual warfare is continuous.** In Romans 12:10, Paul encourages us to continue steadfastly in prayer. *We need more prayer than increased activity.*

Intercessor makes a wall meaning he would restore a breach caused by an enemy. But he would stand in the gap or plug up that breach against that enemy through out the building process.

According to Ezekiel 22:30, God sought for a man among them who would make a wall and stand in the gap before Him on behalf of the land that He should not destroy it: but He found no one.

In Ezekiel day, Judah was all that remained of God's vineyard. His chosen people. The idolatrous kingdom of Israel had been destroyed and the people exited under the Assyrians ruler surgeon in 722 BC

Sin had made a horrendous gap in Judah protective wall. A GAP was a break in the protective thorny hedge or will of stones that surrounded a vineyard and invited trouble. To bar intruders someone had to stand guard until the gap could be repaired.

Therefore the word employs this figure of speech to describe gods search for an intercessor among Judah's priest, prophets, princes or people. For those who would stand in the gap linking god's mercy with mans need.

In our day the protective hedge about familiar, churches and nations is often in a state of terrible – disrepair.

God is still searching for intercessors to stand guard "in the gap" and by prayer to help repair the breaches.

The enemies that have torn down the wall or hedge that tore down the walls in Ezekiel's day still confronts God's people today: lust and immorality, harlotry and idolatry, Oppression and covetousness, greed and hatred, envy and jealousy.

Realizing your power in prayer

According to Ephesians; before you accepted the Lord Jesus as your Savior according to Ephesians you were:

1. Dead in trespasses and sins (anyone born of a woman is born into sin). Meaning you was disconnected from God. We all were sinners. As a result of the fall we lost our dominion and authority. Adam forfeited his dominion and authority to Satan.
2. you once walked according to the power of Satan
3. fulfilled the desires of the flesh and of the mind
4. were by nature children of wrath
5. you were once sinners and without Christ
6. were aliens from the commonwealth of Israel
7. were strangers from the covenant of promise
8. had no hope and without God in this world

But God who is rich in mercy because of his great love with which He loved us made us alive together with Christ. Once we accepted the Lord Jesus as savior being qualified to be partakers of the inheritance of the saints in the light delivered us from the power of darkness and conveyed or transferred us into the kingdom of the son of his love. (Ephesians 4:4-5)

Automatically our dominion and authority were restored. We were instantly rescued from the tyranny of darkness- the negatives as dangers, disease, death and hostile situations in general. He delivered us from both present deliverances and future.

We are now kingdom subjects who have been seated or positioned with Christ far above all principalities, power and might and dominion and every name that is named not only in this age but the age to come.

Principalities and powers and might and dominion are terms consistently used for ruling authorities in both the visible ant the invisible hierarchy of evil powers who deceive and manipulate human behavior thereby advancing satanic strategies. We are placed above these powers that only spiritual warfare can assert, demonstrate, and sustain.

We must understand the warfare is not in the natural but in the spirit. The heavenly place means in the spirit realm. Our struggle is not against flesh and blood but against principalities, powers and rulers of darkness and spiritual wickedness in heavenly places.

So the demonic and satanic manifestation that I see operates in and through a person is only the manifestation of what's going on in the spirit realm. For instance, If Joe curses you, it is not for you to retaliate but to understand that there is an enemy influence and as God's representative you must operate in the Spirit by binding his power or forbidding him to operate in the earth in and through this person and God binds it in the heavenlies. So you partner with God.

Matt 18:18 Verily I say unto you, whatsoever ye shall bind on earth shall be bound in heaven: and whatsoever ye shall loose on earth shall be loosed in heaven.

When we pray from our seat of authority then we can boldly say, No weapon formed against me shall prosper. Weapons against you and me are formed in the spirit realm. When we intervene with prayer it prevents the weapon from prospering. ***Prayer counteracts the onslaught of the enemy.***

We pray the will of God in the situation which is revealed in His word.

God wants you to be strong. So you must take the armor of God and put to use so you will be able to stand up to everything the devil throws your way.

 The Armor of God is an expression that symbolizes the combat equipment of a Christian soldier, who fights against spiritual wickedness; the full resources of God which are available to all who take up the cross and follow Christ. Because our spiritual enemy is stronger than we are, we must put on the whole armor of God (Eph 6:11,13).

1. TRUTH-

Is Conformity to fact or actuality; faithfulness to an original or to a standard.

In the Old and New Testaments, truth is a fundamental moral and personal quality of God. God proclaimed that He is "merciful and gracious, longsuffering, and abounding in goodness and truth" (Ex 34:6). He is a "God of truth...without injustice" (Deut 32:4). Frequently in the Psalms, God's mercy and His truth are joined together (Ps 57:3; 89:14; 115:1).

All of His works, precepts, and judgments are done in righteousness and truth (Ps 96:13; 111:8). The psalmist declared, "Your law is truth" (119:142), "all Your commandments are truth" (119:151), and "the entirety of Your word is truth" (119:160). Because of His perfect nature and will, God speaks and act in truth; He cannot lie (1 Sam 15:29; Heb 6:18; James 1:17-18).

Jesus is the Word of God who became flesh, "the only begotten of the Father, full of grace and truth" (John 1:14). All that Jesus said was true, because He told the truth which He heard from God (John 8:40). He promised His disciples that He would send "the Spirit of truth" (John 14:17; 15:26; 16:13) - a Helper who would abide in Christians forever (John 14:16), testify about Jesus (John 15:26), guide Christians into all truth (John 16:13), and glorify Jesus (John 16:14).God is truth; Jesus is truth; and the Spirit is truth. Jesus said, "I am the way, the truth, and the life. No one comes to the Father except through Me" (John 14:6). Jesus and the revelation which the Spirit of truth gave through His apostles are the final, ultimate revelation and definition of truth about God, man, redemption, history, and the world. "The law was given through Moses, but grace and truth came through Jesus Christ" (John 1:17). Ephesians 6:10-18

Truth or sincerity is our girdle, v. 14. It was prophesied of Christ (Isa 11:5) that righteousness should be the girdle of his loins and faithfulness the girdle of his reins. That with which Christ was girded, the same applies to all Christians. God desires truth, that is, sincerity, in the inward parts. This is the strength of our loins; and it girds on all other pieces of our amour, and therefore is first mentioned. This will restrain from libertinism and licentiousness, as a girdle restrains and keeps in the body. This is the Christian soldier's belt: ungirded with this, he is unblessed.

2. RIGHTEOUSNESS

Is Holy and upright living, in accordance with God's standard. The word righteousness comes from a root word that means "straightness". A moral concept, it refers to a state that conforms to an authoritative standard. God's character is the definition and source of all righteousness (Gen 18:25; Deut 32:4; Rom 9:14). Therefore, man's righteousness is defined in terms of God's. In the Old Testament, righteousness defines man's relationship with God (Ps 50:6; Jer. 9:24) and with other people (Jer. 22:3). In the context of relationships, righteous action is action that promotes the peace and well-being of human beings in their relationships to one another.

For example, Adam and Eve would have acted righteously in their relationship with God if they had obeyed Him, because His commands defined that relationship. The Ten Commandments and related laws defined Israel's relationship with God. To obey those laws was to act righteously, because such obedience maintained the covenant relationship between God and His people. The sacrificial system in the Old Testament and the cross of Jesus in the New Testament show man's need for righteousness.

Man cannot be righteous in the sight of God on his own merits. Therefore, man must have God's righteousness imputed, or transferred to him. The cross of Jesus is a public demonstration of God's righteousness. God accounts or transfers the righteousness of Christ to those who trust in Him (Rom 4:3-22; Gal 3:6; Phil 3:9). We do not become righteous because of our inherent goodness; God sees us as righteous because of our identification by faith with His Son. (Ephesians 6:10-18)

Righteousness must be our breast-plate. The breast-plate secures the vitals and shelters the heart. The righteousness of Christ imputed to us is our breast-plate to protect us from the attacks made by Satan.

The apostle explained, "It is putting on the breast-plate of faith and love." (1 Thess. 5:8), Faith and love include all Christian graces; for by faith we are united to Christ and by love to our brethren. These will infer a diligent observance of our duty to God, and a righteous deportment towards men.

3. PEACE

Ephesians 6:10-18And their feet shod with the preparation of the gospel of peace, shoes, or greaves of brass, or   the like, were formerly part of the military armor (1 Sam 17:6): the use of them was to defend the feet against the gall-traps, and sharp sticks, which were wont to be laid privily in the way, to obstruct the marching of the enemy, those who fell upon them being unfit to march.

The preparation of the gospel of peace signifies a prepared and resolved frame of the mind and heart, to adhere to the gospel and abide by it, which will enable us to walk with a steady pace in the way of religion, notwithstanding the difficulties and dangers that may be encountered. It is styled the gospel of peace because it brings us peace with God, with ourselves, and with one another. It also may mean that which prepares for the entertainment of the gospel, namely, repentance. With this our feet must be shod. For by living a life of repentance we are armed against temptations to sin, and the designs of our great enemy. In the words of Dr. Whitby this may be the sense of the words: "That you may be ready for the combat, be shod with the gospel of peace, endeavor after that peaceable and quiet mind which the gospel calls for. Be not easily provoked, nor prone to quarrel: but show all gentleness and all long-suffering to all men, and this will certainly preserve you from many great temptations and persecutions, as did those shoes of brass the soldiers from those galltraps,"

4. FAITH

Above all Faith must be our shield. Faith is all in all to us in an hour of temptation. The breast-plate secures the vitals; but with the shield we turn every way.

. Consider faith as it is the evidence of things not seen and the substance of things hoped for, and it will appear to be of admirable use for this purpose. Faith, as receiving Christ and the benefits of redemption, so deriving grace from him, is like a shield, a sort of universal defense. We are to be fully persuaded of the truth of all God's promises and such a faith being of great use against temptations Our enemy the devil is called the wicked one. He is wicked himself, and endeavors to make us wicked. His temptations are called darts, because of their swift and undiscerned flight causing deep wounds to the soul.

Violent temptations, by which the soul is set on fire, are the darts which Satan shoots at us. Faith is the shield with which we must quench those fiery darts, when we receive them, and so render them ineffectual, that they do not hit us, or at least that they do not hurt us. Faith, acted upon the word of God and upon the grace of Christ quenches the darts of temptation.

5. SALVATION

Salvation must be our helmet. The helmet secures the head. A good hope of salvation, well founded and well built, will both comfort the soul and keep it from being troubled and tormented by Satan. He would tempt us to despair; but hope keeps us trusting and rejoicing in God.

The word of God is the sword of the Spirit. Just as the sword is a very necessary and useful part of a soldier's gear, The word of God is very necessary, and of great use to the Christian, in order to succeed in spiritual warfare. It is called the sword of the Spirit, because it is of the Spirit's inditing and he renders it efficacious and powerful, and sharper than a two-edged sword. Like Goliath's sword, none like that; with this we assault the assailants. Scripture is the most powerful repellant to temptation. Christ himself resisted Satan's temptations with scriptures. (Matt 4:4, 6, 7, 10) Scriptures hidden in the heart will preserve us from sin (Ps 119:11), and will mortify and kill those latent lusts and corruptions.

6. PRAYER

Prayer must buckle onto all the other parts of our Christian armor, v. 18. We must join prayer with all these graces, for our defense against spiritual enemies, imploring God's assistance as the case requires.

We must pray upon all occasions, and as often as our own and others' necessities call upon us. We must always keep up a disposition to prayer, and should intermix ejaculatory prayers with other duties in our daily walk. We must pray with all prayer and supplication, with all kinds of prayer: public, private, and secret, social and solitary, solemn and sudden; with all the parts of prayer: confession of sin, petition for mercy, and thanksgivings for favors received. We must pray in the Spirit; our spirits must be employed in the duty and we must do it by the grace of God's good Spirit. We must watch thereunto, endeavoring to keep our hearts in a praying frame, and taking all occasions, and improving all opportunities for the duty. When God says, seek my face, our hearts must comply doing this with all perseverance abiding by the duty of prayer. Ps 27:8. Regardless of our circumstances, discouragements and repulses, we must continue in prayer and supplications as long as we live - not for ourselves only, but for all saints; for we are members of one body.

A praying believer is essential in this ongoing warfare.
As believers, we should pray hard and long; praying for your brothers and sisters. Keep your eyes open. Keep each other's spirits up so that no one falls behind or drops out.

Things to Ponder

Who to pray for: 2Kings 19:4

1. Pray for believers John 17:9, 20
2. Pray for authority figures 1Tim 2:2
3. Pray for yourselves
4. Pray for all men 1Tim 2:1
5. Pray for the sick James 5:14

Where to pray:
1. From the temple 2Chron 6:20, Luke 18: 18
2. From your secret place Matt 6:6
3. Pray everywhere 1Tim 2:8

When to pray?
1. Pray always Luke 21: 36
2. Pray without ceasing 1Thess 5:17

What to pray?
1. That you may not enter into temptation Luke 22:40
2. Salvation of others 1Tim 2:4
3. A closer relationship with God

How to pray?
1. Lifting up holy hands 1Tim 2:8
2. Enter into his gates with praise and thanksgiving.
3. Come believing that He is
4. In the Spirit Rom 8:26, 27
5. Pray Specifically

Who should pray?
Those who are godly Psalms 32:6
Through prayer god will instruct and teach you in the way in which you should go. He will guide you with his eye.

PRAYER AND FASTING: THE MASTER KEY TO THE IMPOSSIBLE

Fasting is primarily an act of willing abstinence or reduction from certain or all food, drink, or both, for a period of time. An absolute fast is normally defined as abstinence from all food and liquid for a defined period, usually a single day (24 hours), or several days.

Fasting is generally for religious purposes. It was sometimes done as a sign of distress, grief, or repentance. The Law of Moses specifically required fasting for only one occasion-the DAY OF ATONEMENT. This custom resulted in calling this day "the day of fasting" (Jer 36:6) or "the Fast" (Acts 27:9).

Old and New Testament references to Fasting

Moses did not eat bread or drink water during the 40 days and 40 nights he was on Mount Sinai receiving the law (Ex 34:28). Voluntary group fasts (not specified in the law) were engaged in during time of war, such as when the Benjamites defeated the other Israelites (Judg. 20:26), and when Samuel gathered the people to Mizpah during the Philistine wars (1 Sam 7:6). It was at a called fast that witnesses accused Naboth, setting the stage for his death (1 Kings 21:9, 12).

Jehoshaphat called for a fast in all Israel when opposed by the Moabites and Ammonites (2 Chron.20:3). Reacting to Jonah's preaching, the men of Nineveh, at the king's order, fasted and put on sackcloth (Jonah 3:5). Those about to return with Ezra from captivity fasted at the river of Ahava in the face of the dangers faced on the journey (Ezra 8:21, 23). Esther and the Jews of Shushan (or Susa) fasted when faced with the destruction planned by Haman (Est. 4:3, 16; 9:31).

In times of grief, people fasted. A seven-day fast was held when the bones of Saul and his sons were buried (1 Sam 31:13; 1 Chron. 10:12). Fasting was done during the 70 years of the exilic period on the fifth and the seventh months, the date the siege of Jerusalem began and the date when Jerusalem fell to the Babylonians (Zech 7:5).

Fasting was often done by individuals in times of distress. David fasted after hearing that Saul and Jonathan were dead (2 Sam 1:12). Nehemiah fasted and prayed upon learning that Jerusalem had remained in ruins since its destruction (Neh. 1:4). Darius, the king of Persia, fasted all night after placing Daniel in the lions' den (Dan 6:18).

Going without food or water was not automatically effective in accomplishing the desires of those who fasted. In the prophet Isaiah's time, people complained that they had fasted and that God had not responded favorably (Isa 58:3-4). The prophet declared that the external show was futile. The fast that the Lord requires is to loose the bonds of wickedness, undo the heavy burdens, feed the hungry, shelter the poor, and clothe the naked (Isa 58:5-7).

Fasting also occurs in the New Testament. Anna at the Temple "served God with fasting and prayers night and day" (Luke 2:37). John the Baptist led his disciples to fast (Mark 2:18). Jesus fasted 40 days and 40 nights before His temptation (Matt 4:2). Using a marriage-feast comparison, however, Jesus insisted that fasting was not suitable for His disciples as long as He, the Bridegroom, was with them (Matt 9:14-15; Mark 2:18-20; Luke 5:33-35).

Cornelius was fasting at the time of his vision (Acts 10:30). The church in Antioch fasted (Acts 13:2) and sent Paul and Barnabas off on the first missionary journey with fasting and prayer (Acts 13:3). Paul and Barnabas prayed with fasting at the appointment of elders in the churches (Acts 14:23). Paul suggested that husbands and wives might abstain from sexual intercourse to give themselves to fasting and prayer (1 Cor. 7:5).

FASTING TO BE SEEN BY GOD ONLY
Matt 6:16-18 "Moreover, when you fast, do not be like the hypocrites, with a sad countenance. For they disfigure their faces that they may appear to men to be fasting. Assuredly, I say to you, they have their reward. 17 But you, when you fast, anoint your head and wash your face, 18 so that you do not appear to men to be fasting, but to your Father who is in the secret place; and your Father who sees in secret will reward you openly.

Fast and Pray THAT DEMONIC STRONGHOLDS WILL BE DESTROYED
Matt 17:20-21

20 So Jesus said to them, "Because of your unbelief; for assuredly, I say to you, if you have faith as a mustard seed, you will say to this mountain, 'Move from here to there,' and it will move; and nothing will be impossible for you. 21 However, this kind does not go out except by prayer and fasting."
(NKJV) Mark 2:18-22

Jesus Is Questioned About Fasting
(Matt 9:14-17; Luke 5:33-39)

18 The disciples of John and of the Pharisees were fasting. Then they came and said to Him, "Why do the disciples of John and of the Pharisees fast, but Your disciples do not fast?"

FAST AND PRAY FOR A CLOSER RELATIONSHIP WITH GOD

19 And Jesus said to them, "Can the friends of the bridegroom fast while the bridegroom is with them? As long as they have the bridegroom with them they cannot fast. 20 But the days will come when the bridegroom will be taken away from them, and then they will fast in those days. 21 No one sews a piece of unshrunk cloth on an old garment; or else the new piece pulls away from the old, and the tear is made worse. 22 And no one puts new wine into old wineskins; or else the new wine bursts the wineskins, the wine is spilled, and the wineskins are ruined. But new wine must be put into new wineskins."

Fast AND Pray FOR REVELATION
Acts 10:30-33

30 So Cornelius said, "Four days ago I was fasting until this hour; and at the ninth hour I prayed in my house, and behold, a man stood before me in bright clothing, 31 and said, 'Cornelius, your prayer has been heard, and your alms are remembered in the sight of God. 32 Send therefore to Joppa and call Simon here, whose surname is Peter. He is lodging in the house of Simon, a tanner, by the sea. When he comes, he will speak to you.' 33 So I sent to you immediately, and you have done well to come. Now therefore, we are all present before God, to hear all the things commanded you by God."

FAST AND **PRAY FOR INSTRUCTION**
Acts 14:23-28

23 So when they had appointed elders in every church, and prayed with fasting, they commended them to the Lord in whom they had believed. 24 And after they had passed through Pisidia, they came to Pamphylia. 25 Now when they had preached the word in Perga, they went down to Attalia. 26 From there they sailed to Antioch, where they had been commended to the grace of God for the work which they had completed.

27 Now when they had come and gathered the church together, they reported all that God had done with them, and that He had opened the door of faith to the Gentiles. 28 So they stayed there a long time with the disciples.
NKJV

PRAYER

1.   In general, how would you evaluate the consistency and intensity of your prayers at this time in your life, compared with times in your past? To help you decide, use a scale of one to ten (one = "much less consistent and intense than ever," ten = "much more consistent and intense than ever").

2.   What do you believe is the best definition for the word prayer?

3.   Discuss how the following verses relate to prayer. Take a fresh look at each passage, searching especially for (a) God's commands and standards to keep, (b) someone's example to learn from, (c) a promise from God to believe, (d) a warning to heed, or (e) a challenge to face.
- Deut 4:7
- 1 Sam 12:23
- 1 Kings 18:36-37
- 2 Chron. 7:14
- Neh. 2:4-5
- Ps 5:3; 34:17-18; 42:8; 50:14-15; 88:1,13; 142
- Dan 9:1-23
- Matt 6:5-18; 7:7-8; 18:19-20; 21:22; 26:39
- Mark 1:35
- Luke 11:1-12; 18:1-8
- John 15:7-8
- Eph 6:18
- Col 4:2
- 1 Thess. 5:17
- 1 Tim 2:8

Chapter Eight

THE POWER OF BIBLICAL CHANGE

"For by grace you have been saved through faith; and that not of yourselves, it is the gift of God; not as a result of works, that no one should boast". Eph. 2:8-9 the most significant decision you will ever make concerns your willingness to follow God's plan for your life as revealed in the Bible. This decision directly impacts your daily life and your eternal destiny.

(Scripture references; Psalms 119:165; Prov. 1:33; Matt. 6:25-34; mark 8: 34-38; John 3:16-21; Acts 2:38-39; 2Tim. 3:16-17; 2Peter 1:2-10; Rev. 20:15)

God's plan for you to change in a biblical way centers on His Son, Jesus Christ. Because God's standard is one of perfection (Lev 19:2) you cannot meet it by your own efforts (Psalm143:2; Eccl. 7:20; Rom. 3:23). You cannot save yourself (Prov. 20:9). Nor depend on any other human being to redeem you (Ps. 49:7) You need to recognize your helplessness to meet God's standard (Is.64:6; Rom.3:9-12) and need to repent of your sin (Luke 15:7) Acts 2:38; 3:19, 17:30-31, 26-19-20; Rom. 2:4; 2Pet. 3:9). In the light of this recognition, you are to believe wholeheartedly and sincerely on the Lord Jesus Christ in order to receive forgiveness for your sins (Mark 16:16, Rom. 10:9-13; thus, by God's grace and mercy, you receive the gift of eternal life (Titus 3:1-7; 1John 5:11-13)

The first step to change biblically is simple. You must respond to God's demonstrated love as the necessary first step towards lasting biblical change. (John 1:12, 3:16-21; Rom. 5:8; 2 Cor. 5:17; 1John 4:10)

If you have never taken this first step to change biblically, you can do so right now. Simply tell God you know you are a sinner and need His forgiveness of your sin. Acknowledge to God that neither you nor anyone else but Jesus Christ can save you. Ask God to forgive you of your sin because you know that Jesus died to pay the penalty for sin and rose from the dead so that you might have a new life. By faith, receive the Lord Jesus Christ as Savior and thank God for His grace and love to you through Jesus. With a sincere and repentant heart, demonstrate your commitment to Him by being obedient to His Word.

Secondly, you must understand that man's way of solving problems falls short of God's solutions. The Word of God has been given to man as the sole source for finding God's solutions to the real problems that plague him. (Psalm 19:7-11; 2 Tim. 3:16-17)

It is important to understand the plan of salvation in detail because it is essential that you understand the spiritual principle that all of man's wisdom, philosophy, devices, procedures, manipulations, and sincerity cannot substitute for God's plan of salvation through Jesus Christ. Any person claiming to have taken a different way to salvation except through Jesus Christ is likened in Scripture to a thief and robber (John 10:1, 7)

Thirdly, you need to understand the difference between man's way and God's way in your search for a contented, joyful, and peaceful way of life. The primary difference is that man's way is oriented to self: to please self, to comfort self, to rely on self, to fulfill self, to forgive self, to exalt self, and to love self. This is described in Scripture as the old self-nature (Rom. 6:6; Eph.4:22; Col. 3:9).

However, God's way is to empower, regenerate, and strengthen you to maturity:
   a. Putting off from you the old nature (Rom 6:6, Eph 4:22; Col. 3:9)
   b. Putting on you the new nature (Rom. 6:7-8, Eph 4:24, and
   c. Renewing the spirit of your mind in the continual process to become Christ-like(Rom 12:2: Eph 4:23)
   d. Deny self and follow Jesus (Luke 9:23-24)
   e. Walk in a manner worthy of the Lord (Eph4:1)
   f. Please God in all things (2Cor. 5:9)

Biblical change according to God's plan, instead of man's ideologies (self-focus), establishes your true position in Christ and gives provision for you to be:
   1. Forgiven of all your sins (Col.2:13-14) and become a new creation (2 Cor. 5:17) by partaking of God's divine nature. (2Pet1:4);
   2. A child and heir of God and a joint-heir with Jesus Christ (Rom 8:14-17);
   3. A citizen of heaven(Phil. 3:20), blessed with every spiritual blessing (Eph 1:3) and fully complete in Christ Jesus (Col. 2:9-10);

4. Strong in the Lord(Eph 6:10-17) as a functioning and maturing member of the body of Christ (Eph 4:11-16);
5. More than a conqueror through the Lord Jesus Christ (Rom 8:37; 1john 4:4), since you have been released from sin's slavery(Rom 6:5-7) and have been delivered out of the domain(authority) of darkness and into the kingdom of Christ (Col 1:13)
6. An ambassador for Christ (@Cor.5:20), a member of a chosen race, a royal priesthood, a citizen of a holy nation, a possession of God (1Peter 2:9), and a holy temple of the living God (2 Cor6:16; Eph 2:21)
7. Transformed by the renewing of your mind (Rom 12:2), taking every thought captive to the obedience of Christ (@ Corinthians 10:5);
8. Full of His peace (John 16:33) and joy (John 15:11, 17:13);
9. Changed by His Word (1Thess. 2:13; 2 Tim. 3:16-17);
10. Led by the Spirit of God (Rom. 8:14) to understand the things of God. (1Cor 2:9-13);
11. Able to accomplish(or endure) anything in God's will for you through Christ Jesus (Philippians 4:13), knowing that God is in total control of your life (Rom. 8:28-29; 1Cor 10:13; Philippians 1:6); and
12. Empowered to practice biblical love, thus proving yourself to be a disciple of Christ.

Since God has graciously provided everything that is necessary for you to live a life pleasing to Him, you are to depend solely on His power, plan, and resources to accomplish His purpose in your life.

Further Biblical References Related to Women

Woman - the female sex
A. Described as:

Beautiful ……. 2 Sam. 11:2
Wise ………… 2 Sam. 20:6
Widow………..1Kin. 17:9, 10
Evil…………..Prov. 6: 24
Foolish………..Job 2:10
Gracious……..Prov.11:16
Virtuous……..Prov. 12: 4
Contentious….Prov. 21:19
Adulterous…..Prov. 30: 20
Honorable……Acts 17: 12
Silly………….2 Tim. 3:6
Holy………….1Pet 3:5

B. Work of:

Kneading meal……Gen. 18:6
Drawing water……Gen. 24:11, 13, 15
Tending sheep…….Gen. 29:6
Making cloth………Prov. 31:13, 19
Caring for household…Prov. 31:27, 1Tim 5:14

C. Rights to:

Marry….. 1Cor. 7:36
Hold property…..Num. 27:6-11
Make vows……..Num 30:3-9

D. Position of, in relation to man:

Created from man..........Gen. 2: 21-25
Made to help man..........Gen. 2:18, 20
Glory to man................1Cor. 11:7-9
Becomes subject to man....Gen. 3:16
Weaker than man...........1Pet. 3:16

E. Position in Spiritual things:

Insight of, noted.........Judg. 13:23
Prayer of, answered.....1Sam. 1:9-28
Understanding of rewarded...1Sam. 25:3-42
Faith of, brings salvation....Luke 7:37-50
Made equal in Christ.........Gal. 3:28
Labor of, commended.......Phil. 4:2, 3
Faith of, transmitted.........2 Tim 1:5

F. Good Traits of:

Obedience..........1Pet. 3:5-7
Concern for children.... Ex. 2:2-10
Loyalty..............Ruth 1: 14-18
Desire for children.......1Sam. 1:9-28
Modesty..............Ruth 1:10-12
Industry..............Prov. 31: 10-31
Complete devotion....Luke 7: 38-50
Tenderness............John 11:20-35

G. Bad Traits of:

Inciting to evil..........Gen. 3: 6, 7
Subtle...................Prov. 7: 10
Fond of adornments....Is. 3:16-24
Self-indulgent............Is. 32:9, 11
Easily led into idolatry.... Jer. 7: 18
Led away...................2 Tim. 3: 6

H. Prohibitions concerning, not to:

Wear man's clothing........Deut. 22:5
Have head shaved..........1 Cor. 11:5-15
Usurp authority..............1Tim. 2:11-15
Be unchaste...................1Pet. 3:1-7

www.ingramcontent.com/pod-product-compliance
Lightning Source LLC
LaVergne TN
LVHW021522080426
835509LV00018B/2605